ICKENHAM & HAREFIELD PAST

First published 1996
by Historical Publications Ltd
32 Ellington Street, London N7 8PL
(Tel: 0171-607 1628)

ISBN 0 948667 36 2
British Library Cataloguing-in-Publication Data
A catalogue record for this book is available from the British Library

Typeset in Palatino by Historical Publications Ltd
Reproduction by G & J Graphics, London EC2
Printed by Edelvives in Zaragoza, Spain

Historical Publications Ltd specialises in local history publishing.
A full list of its publications may be obtained on application.
With few exceptions they are all distributed by Phillimore & Co,
Shopwyke Manor Barn, Chichester, Sussex PO20 6BG.

The publishers would be happy to receive proposals for other
titles in this series.

ICKENHAM & HAREFIELD PAST

a Visual History

by Eileen M. Bowlt

HISTORICAL PUBLICATIONS

Contents

Introduction

As the second millennium approaches, Ickenham and Harefield present entirely different pictures to the world. Ickenham is suburban in appearance and outlook, while Harefield is more at ease with its rural past, retaining a farming community and with an ancient church still set amid fields. Neither view is entirely true.

Ickenham's pleasant tree-lined closes and roads are obvious to those who drive through it, but they screen such scenes of past glory as the 14th-century Pynchester moated site; Manor Farm, also dating in part from the mid-14th century; and the mellow beauty of Swakeleys. Such gems are best discovered on foot. Even as a suburb, Ickenham has some strange omissions. Where, for example, was the cinema, so essential to a comfortable life in the 1930s? Ickenham in fact is a suburb whose development was arrested by the passing of the Green Belt legislation in the late 1930s. Prior to that plans had been drawn for Francis Jackson Developments, to build a Manor Homes estate in the fields around Ickenham Marsh. It would have been similar to Ruislip Manor. (A few Manor Homes did appear in Glebe Avenue.) A major road was intended to continue south from the bottom of Austins Lane across the Yeading Brook towards Sharvel Lane. A cinema, two schools and several shopping areas were envisaged spreading over the fields of Hill Farm, and a tiny area on either side of the Yeading was labelled 'green belt' and left for recreation. None of this development took place (except for the building of Glebe School) and Northolt Aerodrome expanded out of Ruislip across Hill Farm on the south side of the brook during the Second World War. The area, which contains many interesting plants, remains open for walkers and naturalists to enjoy.

So far as Harefield is concerned, it is the industrial past along the river and canal that has disappeared, to be replaced by housing, office developments and small commercial concerns. Ever more housing estates are being built in the grounds of old mansions and farms, like Harefield House and Manor Court. Despite the enlarged population there are slightly fewer pubs than there once were and there has been no major shopping development. Like their forbears the people of Harefield travel to Uxbridge, Rickmansworth and Watford to shop.

Harefield has made its mark on the modern world because of the pioneering work on heart surgery and heart and lung transplants by Doctor Magdi Yacoub at Harefield Hospital, the former Harefield Park. The hospital that was founded during the First World War to nurse Australian soldiers, now attracts patients from Europe and Asia.

This book highlights the life and work and houses of the people of these two parishes from the time of the Domesday Book to the late 20th century with the aid of numerous pictures. Details left out of the explanatory text may be found in the books mentioned in the notes on pp. 140-1.

1. *Ickenham village in the early years of this century. From the left can be seen Little Buntings, St Giles's church, the pump with the pond behind, the Fox and Geese, Home Farm, the cottages beside the pond with a row of cottages behind them, once called Hollywood Row. All these buildings remain except for Hollywood Row, but the church was extended in 1958 and the Fox and Geese has been rebuilt.*

The Two Parishes

Harefield is often referred to as the last village in Middlesex because of the number of working farms still to be found there at the end of the twentieth century. It nestles in the north-west corner of the county, separated from Hertfordshire and Buckinghamshire by the Colney Stream, the shire ditch and the River Colne. The parish of Hillingdon and the market town of Uxbridge lie immediately south. The eastern boundary marches with the fields and woods of Ruislip as far as the River Pinn, where it meets Ickenham. The close proximity of the M25 has put increasing pressure upon Harefield in recent years and an unprecedented amount of building has taken place since 1980, making it ever more suburban in character; but the fact that no permanent railway station has yet penetrated the parish still marks it as different from the rest of modern Middlesex.

Ickenham is much smaller than Harefield (1,458 acres opposed to 4,621 acres before twentieth-century boundary changes) but being more densely built up has a larger population: 11,438 people were recorded in Ickenham at the 1991 census and about 6,500 in Harefield. Ickenham adjoins its larger neighbour on the south-east. Nowadays it is unashamedly a London suburb, but one with a 'village centre' and many reminders of its fairly recent rural past, including a small mainly medieval church and a village pump.

In the days when counties were divided into Hundreds for administrative purposes, both places were in the Hundred of Elthorne. Both became part of Uxbridge Rural District in 1894 and subsequently Uxbridge Urban District in 1929. Since 1965 they have been in the Borough of Hillingdon.

THE EARLY INHABITANTS

Harefield and Ickenham make their first appearance in written records in the Domesday Book of 1086, from which we learn that there were late Saxon settlements in both places. Ickenham is flattish, varying between 101ft and 136ft above sea-level. Apart from alluvium along the Pinn the soil is London Clay, a material that has generally been untouched by commercial excavation in modern times, except for the digging of house foundations. The sites of new houses have only recently been watched for archaeological finds and consequently very little evidence of early habitation has yet been found. A dig undertaken by MOLAS (Museum of London Archaeological Services) in a playing field east of Long Lane, only a quarter of a mile from the Ickenham parish boundary, in the autumn of 1994, uncovered part of a system of Romano-British fields, cultivated in the 1st and 2nd century AD. A scatter of pottery suggested that the farmhouse was nearby.

2. Geological map of Ickenham (drawn by D.F.A. Kiddle).

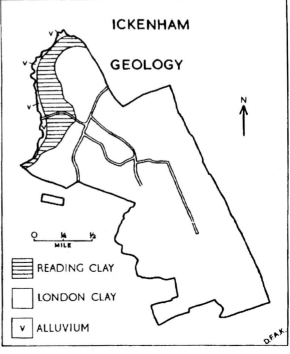

ICKENHAM

GEOLOGY

N

```
0      ¼      ½
        MILE
```

READING CLAY

LONDON CLAY

v ALLUVIUM

D.F.A.K.

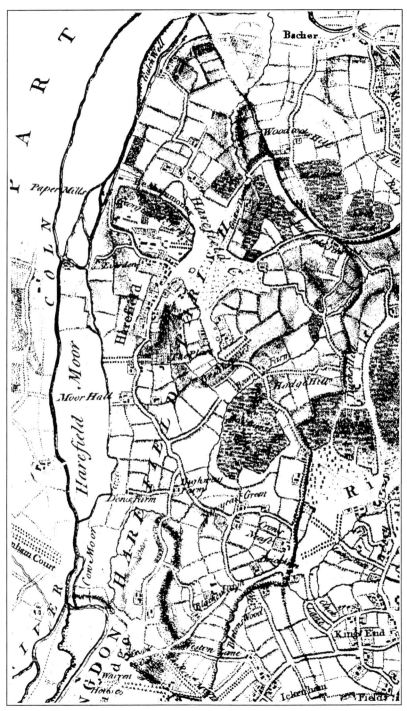

3. Harefield Parish in the north-west corner of Middlesex, as drawn on Rocque's map of the county dated 1754. Gulchwell is now known as Springwell.

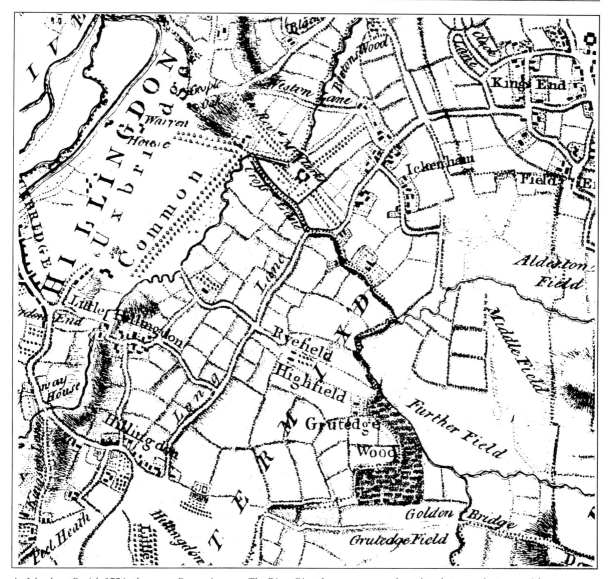

4. *Ickenham Parish 1754, shown on Rocque's map. The River Pinn forms a common boundary between the two parishes.*

Harefield, situated on one side of the Colne, also has predominantly London Clay, with a gravel capped plateau at the top of the steep hill, surrounded by Reading Beds and alluvium and chalk on the valley side. The highest point is 325ft. Gravel extraction since the 1960s has destroyed the former moors (wet places), but has created gravel pits, now used for recreation and scenically attractive. The Colne Valley has produced a good deal of evidence of early man. The earliest finds are Acheulian hand axes used by hunting parties between 250,000 and 200,000 BC. As

they were in an abraded condition, they were probably rolled some distance from the hunters' camps. Flint flakes, scrapers and part of an axe from two sites near Dewes Farm on the moors beside the river, date from the Mesolithic period (8,500-4,500 BC). Neolithic polished flint stone axes have been found along the Colne as well as Bronze Age flint-tempered pottery.[1]

The only reputed Roman finds in Harefield are away from the valley and near Breakspears, where Roman 'sepulchres' were discovered in 1818 and a portion of Roman road was examined in the 1950s.

5. *A view across Moorhall Gravel Pit, Harefield, to the Fisheries Estate, Denham in 1981. The area covered by water was formerly part of Harefield Moor.*

The whole area may have suffered some sort of decline after the Romans left Britain, for nothing has been found to suggest continuous settlement in this area until the mid-11th century vills mentioned in the Domesday Book.

THE DOMESDAY OWNERS

The pre-Conquest owners of these lands were people of standing in Saxon England. Harefield was a single estate and the Countess Goda who held it, was the sister of Edward the Confessor. Both her husbands were French, Dreux of the Vexin and Count Eustace of Boulogne. Ickenham, referred to as Ticheham, was owned by five men and was obviously composed of a group of separate estates. Earl Leofwin was a brother of King Harold;   Toki and Ulf, were housecarls (members of the king's bodyguard) and Ansgar held the position of staller (an official) in Edward the Confessor's household; Wlward Wit was a major landowner with property in at least ten other counties. Neighbouring Ruislip belonged to him and his Ickenham lands, farmed by three of his men, may have been small freehold estates chopped from the main Ruislip property. Similarly, Ansgar's Ickenham land could once have been attached to his Northolt estate.

After the Conquest Harefield, then described as a manor, passed to Richard FitzGilbert, son of Count Gilbert of Brionne. The Ickenham estates were taken over by three Normans. A manor composed of Toki's, Ulf's and part of Wlward's land was owned by Earl Roger, a cousin of William the Conqueror. Earl Leofwin and Ansgar's land went to Geoffrey de Mandeville, Sheriff of Middlesex and chief officer of the City of London. The two Englishmen to whom he let it may have been the former farmers under Leofwin and Ansgar. Wlward's other land was taken by Robert Fafiton.

Earl Roger's manor later included at least part of Geoffrey de Mandeville's land and the two together seem to have become the medieval manor of Ickenham. Robert Fafiton's small estate probably developed into Swakeleys.

ASSESSING THE LAND

The picture of Harefield that emerges from the few lines written in the Domesday Book, is of a well-watered and wooded landscape, with more arable land (sufficient for five ploughs to work) than meadow (one plough), and pasture on which livestock was raised. The woodland here as elsewhere in Middlesex was measured by the number of pigs it could support. Harefield's 1200 pigs gave it more woodland than anywhere else in the Hundred of Elthorne except Ruislip (1500 pigs). The Colne was clearly of great importance to the manor, as it supported two watermills, probably on the site of Springwell and

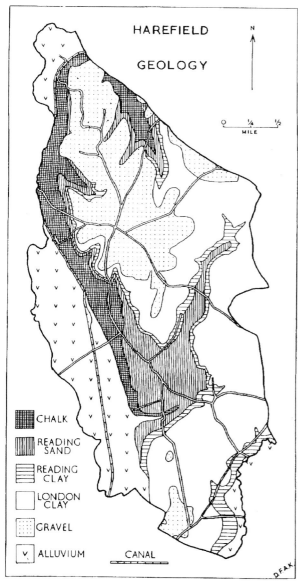

HAREFIELD

GEOLOGY

N

¼   ½
MILE

CHALK

READING SAND

READING CLAY

LONDON CLAY

GRAVEL

ALLUVIUM

CANAL

D.F.A.K.

6. Geological map of Harefield (drawn by D.F.A. Kiddle).

the present Coppermills; and was presumably the source of the eels that stocked the four fish ponds also mentioned.

The Ickenham estates had more meadow than Harefield (enough for seven ploughs) and arable land (six ploughs and three more possible), pasture for domestic animals and enough woodland for forty pigs. On the face of it this seems odd, as Ickenham covers a much smaller area than Harefield, but the discrepancy may partially be accounted for by the unspecified amounts of pasture and the fact that Harefield had apparently thirty times more woodland than Ickenham.

The assessment of Ickenham, as having six times as much meadow as Harefield, could mean that one of the Ickenham Domesday estates, (perhaps the part of Geoffrey de Mandeville's land that had belonged to Ansgar the Staller before the Conquest), covered the southern part of Harefield and stretched down to the Colne. Part of the wasteland at the southern end of Harefield above the Colne and sweeping down to the Pinn, near the present Harefield Place, was known as Northolt Common as late as the eighteenth century[2], and both Ansgar and Geoffrey had owned Northolt in the eleventh century. (Some of the same waste was in Hillingdon and is now called Uxbridge Common.) Brackenbury, close by, was a freehold estate with manorial status in medieval times, regarded as a sub-manor of Harefield. If it had passed from Ickenham into Harefield at an early date, before Ickenham had a church and became an independent parish, some of the anomalies would be explained.

There is, however, a further puzzle in that Harefield was assessed for taxation at only five hides, whereas the Ickenham estates together answered for fifteen. A hide was notionally the amount of land that could be ploughed by an ox team in a year and support a family; it came to be recognised as an area consisting of between 80 and 120 acres. There is no obvious reason why Ickenham should have been assessed so much more highly than Harefield with its mills and fishponds, but a possible explanation may lie in the Domesday entry for Earl Roger's manor, where it says:

"Now the whole of this land lies in Colham, where it was not before 1066".

Colham and Hillingdon were intermingled in the eleventh century and shared a boundary with Ickenham. All belonged to Earl Roger. It would be easy for Ickenham land to have been subsumed in Hillingdon. Confusion continued. In 1453 the Bishop of Worcester, who was rector of Hillingdon, sued the rector of Ickenham for collecting "the tithes of a certain place called Tykenham, which the said Rectors of Ickenham had for some years received, as belonging to their parish, but by this sentence, the

7. *A view taken in 1985 from Rickmansworth Road, Harefield, looking across Dellfield (where chalk was dug) and Lower Woodcocks, showing the still wooded landscape.*

said lands were pronounced to be within the parish of Hillingdon".[3]   Oldberry Woods and the lands forming Long Lane Farm, although lying in Hillingdon, were part of Ickenham manor in the eighteenth century.

MEDIEVAL PEOPLE

Reference is made in Domesday to a priest in Harefield which means that there was a church there. There was no priest in Ickenham so the people must have gone to the churches of Harefield, Ruislip or Colham (on the site of the present St John's on Hillingdon Hill).

Altogether, 25 people were said to be living in Harefield, three of them being slaves. The priest has a virgate (quarter of a hide) of land. There were ten 'villeins' (tenants) who at that time probably held their land freely from the lord in return for rent and labour services but who, by the twelfth or thirteenth century had become unfree, though not necessarily poor men, and tied to their lords. Seven 'bordars' (poorer tenants) with five acres each and one with three acres, were probably smallholders and superior in status to the three 'cottars' who probably had little

more than a cottage and garden. Apart from the slaves, the folk mentioned were probably heads of households, so the population of Harefield must have been in the region of 100. Exactly the same numbers of people are enumerated in Ickenham (thirteen villeins, nine bordars, three cottars) producing a similar total population.

THE LANDSCAPE

Until modern times Harefield had heathland on the gravelly plateau on the top of the hill, moors used for grazing along the Colne and scattered farms with enclosed fields along the roads leading to Rickmansworth, Northwood, Ruislip and Uxbridge. The usual system of open common fields, divided into strips, does not seem to have been established in Harefield, although there are references in manorial rentals to two common fields, Hill Field and North Field during the sixteenth century. These lay on the chalky slope above the Colne, north of Coppermills, and seem to have been cultivated by a limited number of people; they had disappeared by the eighteenth century, perhaps becoming incorporated in Old Park Wood. There were two large

8. The thatched lodge in Harvil Road at the entrance to Harefield Place stands on land formerly known as Bungers Hill Common "adjoining Northolt Common or Uxbridge Common".

tracts of woodland, Bayhurst (90 acres) first mentioned in 1221 and Old Park Wood (60 acres) and innumerable small pieces of woodland, several like Scarlet Spring on the hill above Bourne Farm, being named in the fourteenth century.

Part of the gravelly plateau covering the highest part of Harefield remained heathland until the enclosure of the waste in 1813, but the rest had been gradually brought under cultivation ·in medieval times. Thomas de Luda, whose name survives in Loudswood Fields behind Knightscote Farm, was granted several pieces of heath to enclose at the beginning of the fourteenth century. He and his wife Florence had to give a clove gillyflower for a piece in front of his messuage, probably the original Knightscote, and a rose for a piece in front of his wood as token rent.[4] This enclosure, however, displeased other Harefield people and an agreement was drawn up in 1316 and sealed by 44 free tenants, permitting them to throw down the dyke built around his land, if he attempted any further enclosure.

The pattern of early settlement in Harefield is a little uncertain. The present centre is at the cross roads at the top of the hill, on the edge of the plateau gravels, but the twelfth-century parish church is nearly

a mile away down the appropriately named Church Hill, close to the site of the first manor house, but still high above the Colne. It stands physically in the centre of the parish. The large, rough field in front of it and manor house was called Sudbury (Southbury), which may be an indication that it was the site of the original village, or of the southern of two settlements. It might have been cleared for the creation of a home park by Simon de Swanlond, lord of the manor from 1315. Court rolls show that houses were spreading up the hill, encroaching upon the heath in the sixteenth and seventeenth centuries. Hamlets at Hill End and New Years Green were well established by the seventeenth century.

The village of Ickenham clusters around the church at the junction of the Uxbridge, Ruislip and Hillingdon roads. The present church was built early in the fourteenth century, probably on the site of a thirteenth-century chapel, to serve a small settlement already in existence at the junction. There were a number of isolated buildings in medieval times, including the manor house and Swakeleys, both situated near to the parish boundary. A small settlement developed at Ickenham Green in the nineteenth century. Two lanes, now called Austins Lane and

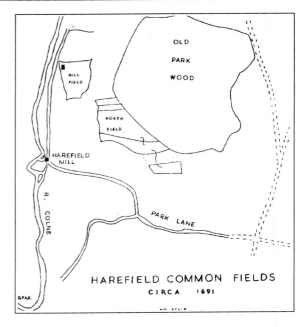

9. (Top) Long Lane Farm from Hillingdon Station bridge, Long Lane in 1982, showing lands in Hillingdon parish that were once part of Ickenham. The new slip roads for the A40 have swallowed up some of these fields in recent years.

10. (Above) A small settlement developed at the south-eastern end of Ickenham Green in the 1820s when the Soldier's Return was built and one or two modern houses have been added more recently.

11. (Above) Harefield Common fields in the late seventeenth century (drawn by D.F.A. Kiddle).

12. (Below) The hamlet of Hill End c.1920. The Vernon Arms (demolished) and cottages on the right were built on former heathland after the 1813 enclosures. They replaced the seventeenth-century cottages that stood on the Long Field behind. The pond was called the Sheep Washing pond. Town End Farm (demolished) can be seen on the left. Its earlier name was Chownes. A Quaker called John Wheeler lived there at the end of the seventeenth century.

13. *Knightscote Farm Cottages, Breakspear Road in 1929 (demolished). They stood on the former heath enclosed by Thomas de Luda in 1311. The pond is believed to be a kiln pond, created by digging clay for brickmaking in the seventeenth or eighteenth century.*

14. *St Leonard's Farm at New Years Green owes its present name to a jocular reference to Leonard Ritchie, whose father bought the farm in 1921. It was known as Marlwards in the sixteenth century when the hamlet consisting of about six houses was called Newes. The eighteenth-century facade built onto the older house contains interesting sliding windows. The photograph was taken in 1980 when the whole farm was less dilapidated than it is today.*

Glebe Avenue, led into the open fields to the south-east. There were three large fields, Home, Middle and Further Fields and two smaller ones, Bleak or Black Hill and Tottingworth Field. Western Avenue now cuts across the former common fields and some have become part of Northolt Aerodrome.

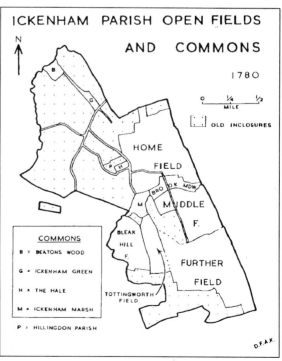

15. *Map of the common fields of Ickenham (drawn by D.F.A. Kiddle).*

The Manors of Ickenham

There were two manors in Ickenham, the manor of Ickenham itself and a submanor, Swakeleys.

ICKENHAM MANOR

The Shorediches were lords of the manor of Ickenham from the mid-fourteenth century until 1819. Before that Ickenham manor was treated as part of Earl Roger's fief, some at least of the de Mandeville lands apparently having become part and parcel of the same. In 1334, John Charlton, a London merchant took possession. He came to own Hillingdon and Cowley Hall as well before 1348 and his son, another John Charlton, had Swakeleys by 1350. The manor of Ickenham was left to his daughter Juette and passed into the hands of the Shorediche family through her marriage to Nicholas Shorediche c.1348. Ickenham finally stood alone, separate from Hillingdon, but the common overlordship of former times may account for the strange position of the manor house just within the boundary with Hillingdon.[1]

The present house, reached down a track from Long Lane, is called Manor Farm, but until the nineteenth century was known as Ickenham Hall. Recent investigation of the building construction suggests that the rear wing is part of an open hall that possibly dates from the mid-fourteenth century and could therefore have been built at the time of Juette's marriage.[2] A cross-wing, partly destroying the hall was added in the early sixteenth century, a three-storey staircase wing was erected in the next century and two small brick parlours were built onto the front in the eighteenth century. The hall was possibly surrounded by an inner moat. Two arms of what must have been the large outer moat remain, now part of Douay Martyrs School playing fields. The area is very low-lying, close to the Yeading Brook and a moat would have been necessary for drainage apart from being a fashionable adjunct to the house. It could also have formed a cattle enclosure, provided a useful water supply and some measure of defence.

16. *Ickenham Manor photographed in Edwardian times. It was known as Ickenham Hall until about 1820, after which date it became Manor Farm. The oldest part of the building can just be seen on the extreme left. The eighteenth-century brick parlours are at the front of the house on the right.*

ICKENHAM, THE MANOR FARM

17. *The three-storey staircase wing added to the manor house can be seen on the left and the surviving portion of the possibly mid-fourteenth century hall is in the centre, partially obscured by the tree.*

THE SHOREDICHES[3]

The Shorediches were people of account in the four-teenth century. Juette's husband accompanied his father beyond the seas on the King's service in 1335. John, his father, an advocate of the ecclesiastical Court of Arches, had been appointed ambassador to treat with Philip of France about a marriage between Edward III's sister and Prince John. Nicholas had lands in Hackney, Stepney and Shoreditch, whence the family took their name. His grandson John was Sheriff of London in 1405. The Shorediches contin-ued in quiet possession of Ickenham for some 450 years, improving their house and farming the de-mesne (land retained for his own use by the lord of the manor) that varied in size from time to time, but was usually about 100 acres in extent, until the family fell on hard times in the late eighteenth century. It was then composed of Manor Farm, Long Lane Farm and Cannons Farm (demolished, with Edinburgh Drive now on site).

Paul Rycaut Shorediche (1790-1850), writing to his eldest son about 1830, explained how the Ickenham property was lost.

"My grandfather [Richard Shorediche 1713-48] mar-ried his first cousin Jane Shorediche. He died soon after my father was born, who was thus left to the care of a very amiable but weak woman. As my father was the only one of the name, he was brought up in every luxury and completely spoiled. He was sent to College as a gentleman of means among noblemen and men of rank and fortune. To compete with them he mortgaged and sold all the lands not entailed and at last sold his life interest in that wise. To redeem his fortune he married my mother who was daughter and co-heiress of Col Edward Rycaut..."

The Rycaut property was in the West Indies, but any fortune gained was frittered away in litigation set in motion by Paul's sister and her husband Gen-eral O'Brien and the Ickenham property was put up for sale in 1815 and finally conveyed in 1818 to George Robinson, a Richmond builder who was rising in the world.[4] Thereafter the hall was let to farmers and known as Manor Farm.

Paul Rycaut Shorediche's sons had to make their own way and sought a living abroad. One was murdered in the Australian gold-rush; another was

18. *Long Lane Farm pictured in 1922. The lands attached to the farm, although in Hillingdon parish, were part of Ickenham. The house is first mentioned as the "messuage in Hillingdon" in articles of agreement drawn up in 1710 when the Revd John Shorediche was about to marry Ann Walton. It had probably been built a few years earlier. There is a dated brick by the door with 'J.S. 1700' on it. After the Shorediche's financial troubles the farm passed to John Hambrough in the 1820s. William Capel Clarke-Thornhill purchased it in 1869 bringing it into the Swakeleys estate. Edward Dalton, the tenant farmer from 1906, bought it at the 1922 auction and it is still a working farm belonging to Dalton's Dairies Ltd.*

19. *These cottages, which stand end on to Long Lane, were sometimes called Cannons Cottages and were sold as part of Cannons Farm in 1859. Their date is uncertain. Probably they were rebuilt using old materials, perhaps taken from Ryefields Farm when it was demolished in the late 1860s. The photograph was taken in 1982. They stand empty and forlorn in 1995 awaiting refurbishment and an estate of detached houses is to be erected on their gardens.*

drowned at sea; two lived and died in Antigua, where Edward, the recipient of his father's letter, was Inspector-General of Police. He returned to England and visited Ickenham in July 1859, where, as he wrote to his sister, he received "...a hearty reception from all the old farmers..." George Robinson had died in 1852 and his estate, having become the subject of a Chancery suit, was ordered to be sold. The auction that included Ickenham Manor had just taken place a few days before and the lands had been "...purchased by Mr Clarke at half their value..." If Edward Shorediche had been hoping to salvage something from the wreck of the family fortunes he was doomed to disappointment, for he checked George Robinson's title and found it good. Further annoyance was in store, when he visited St Giles's church and discovered that the rector, Mr Addison, had either removed or covered up several tablets commemorating his ancestors. By a happy coincidence a descendant, Capt. P.R. de Shorediche Churchward, purchased Manor Farm in 1950 and sold it to Sir Peter Tizard, another descendant in 1961. Humphrey Tizard and his family now reside there. Edward would have been pleased!

The Mr Clarke who got such a bargain in 1859 was Thomas Truesdale Clarke of Swakeleys.

SWAKELEYS MANOR

Swakeleys was a manor, although subordinate to Ickenham. The estate is believed to have grown out of Robert Fafiton's Domesday holding. The name comes from an early fourteenth-century owner, Robert Swalcliffe of Swalcliff, Oxfordshire. In 1350 it was taken over by John Charlton, Juette Shorediche's brother. A later Charlton died fighting on the wrong side at Bosworth in 1485 and although his widow was allowed to retain a life interest, Henry VII then granted Swakeleys to Sir Thomas Bourchier. The manor changed hands several times between 1510-31, passing from Bourchier to Sir John Pecche, to Henry Courtenay, Earl of Devon, then to Ralph Pexall. It stayed with the Pexalls and their descendants through the female line until 1595.[5]

Robert Bromley, a London draper, was the next owner. He leased it to William Cragg, an Attorney of the Court of Common Pleas, in 1606, shortly before selling it to John Bingley. William Cragg's tenancy was to run until 1627. Robert Bromley happened also to be a trustee of nearby Brackenbury, held on behalf of Winifred, John Newdigate's widow and William Cragg had been living there up to 1602.

Trouble between landlord and tenant gave rise to Exchequer proceedings in 1616.[6] The papers give a clear picture of the house at that time. It stood within a moat. A "Great Chamber and Room...called the King's Chamber, with an inner chamber thereunto..." was excepted from the lease and Robert Bromley had the use of a kitchen, buttery, hall and great parlour as well, along with stabling for his horses. He paid for the hay. He and his steward and tenants were allowed to hold the Swakeleys manor courts there.

These rights passed to John Bingley, but about 1614, after he had spent a great deal of money building a brick wall about the house and gardens, repairing the buildings, replanting an orchard and damming up the moat because the water was "corrupt and unhealthful", William Cragg, "a man of turbulent condition", prevented him from using the Great Chamber and other rooms. William Cragg's answer to the complaint told a very different story; of damaged pasture, uprooted fruit-bearing trees, flooded rooms because the water courses had been stopped up and loss of water from the moat, so sweet that it "did serve for dressing of food, drink, washing and other necessary offices." The fifty workmen building the wall had driven away all but three of the 120 pairs of pigeons in the ancient dovehouse. Mr Bingley had even had a four-acre close dug up to make 800,000 bricks. The end of this sad affair is not known, but John Bingley remained in possession until 1629, when he sold Swakeleys to Sir Edmund Wright of the Grocers' Company, Alderman and later Lord Mayor of London.

The grand house described was probably fairly old by 1616, as an inventory taken in 1465 when Sir Thomas Charlton had died, seems to refer to the same rooms. It is impossible to say whether this was the first house built at Swakeleys. There was a park surrounding the house by the fifteenth century.

THE NEW MANSION

Sir Edmund Wright built a new mansion for himself, the rather splendid one that still stands in Swakeleys Park. The work was complete by 1638, the date on the rainwater heads. The house is Jacobean in style, built in brick on an H plan, with unconventional classical details. A notable interior feature is the hall screen, put in by Sir James Harrington, Edmund Wright's son-in-law after the latter's death in 1643. Catherine Harrington had inherited under her father's will, which recommended that she should entertain her relatives there for a fortnight each year. The screen of wood, with columns painted to look like marble, is believed to be the work of John Colt[7] (nephew of the sculptor Maximilian Colt whose tomb of Lady Alice, Dowager Countess of Derby can be seen in Harefield church) and may have been created for another place, as it is slightly too tall for the space: lions on either side of the broken pediment scrape the ceiling with their heads! Placed upon the screen were busts of King Charles I, Lords Essex and Fairfax and on the other side, the parson of the parish, the lord of the manor and his sisters. This choice amused Samuel Pepys when he saw the screen on his visit to Swakeleys in 1665, for Sir James was a Long Parliament man and had been a judge at Charles I's trial. He had to flee the country when Charles II was restored to the throne in 1660. Lady Harrington

20. *Swakeleys, the slightly old-fashioned mansion built for Sir Edmund Wright in 1638. Bricks are used throughout the construction. Even the pediments, cornices and string courses are of brick covered with plaster to simulate stone.*

21. *The entrance hall shown in 1909, when the Gilbey family were living at Swakeleys. King Charles I's bust still presides on top of the wooden screen, as it did when Samuel Pepys saw it in 1665. The panelling and marble fireplace were probably installed by Sir Robert Vyner at about that time.*

22. *The saloon occupies the whole of the centre of the first floor. It was known as the Long Gallery in Vyner's time and here Pepys was entertained by the singing of Mrs Worship, a fellow guest, "very neatly – to my great delight."*

stayed on for a time, but the house was sold to Sir Robert Vyner who was living there in September 1665. Sir Robert Clayton may have contemplated buying it just before and was there in August when his wife gave birth to their only son, who died on the same day and is buried with a pathetic monument in St Giles.

Pepys, who visited Swakeleys twice to borrow money from Sir Robert, a goldsmith, on behalf of the king, thought highly of it: "...it is a place not very moderne in the garden nor house, but the most uniforme in all that ever I saw; and some things to excess." Sir Robert showed him as a curiosity "....a black boy he had, that died of a consumption, and being dead, he caused him to be dried in an oven, and lies there entire in a box." Sir Robert died in 1688, leaving Swakeleys to his nephew Thomas, whose son – another Robert Vyner – sold it to Benjamin Lethieullier and his sister-in-law, Sarah Lethieullier in 1741.

The purchase was on behalf of the widowed Sarah's 12-year-old son, Benjamin. The Lethieulliers owned Belmont in Uxbridge (Belmont Road), a house in Fenchurch Street and estates in Hertfordshire. As soon as Benjamin attained his majority in 1750 he sold the property to the Revd Thomas Clarke, rector of Ickenham since 1747, whose descendants remained in possession until 1922.

THE CLARKES OF SWAKELEYS

The house, park and deer, the lead pipes and conduit from a water house on Uxbridge Common and timber in the park, goods and furniture, cost Mr Clarke £7,100. The sale took place in February, but he was unable to move in immediately because the tenant, Mrs Serle had been promised that she should stay until mid-summer and Mr Lethieullier did not think it quite honourable to insist that she should leave earlier. He ended a friendly letter to Mr Clarke: "All here join me with compliments to you and Mrs Clarke and whenever you take a ride to town, should be very glad if you would make this your Baiting place and take a bitt of Dinner with us."[8]

The Clarkes were newly wed and anxious to move into their new house. Mary Clarke, formerly Mary Blencowe, was an inspectress for the Foundling Hospital and organised the fostering of foundlings among the cottagers of Ickenham. After her death in 1771 her husband married Frances Truesdale from Harefield Place. The eldest son of this second marriage was called Thomas Truesdale Clarke (1774-1840) and he succeeded his father to Swakeleys in 1796. He became an active and influential magistrate and increased his estate.

He had a strange death, being found lying on his back in the River Pinn, within his own park, in only 20 inches of water, his body not being covered with

23. *Thomas Truesdale Clarke (1774-1840), who was drowned in the River Pinn in 1840.*

water, only his face. He had not been himself for some weeks, but an inquest jury held at Swakeleys forbore to bring in a verdict of suicide, which in fact had not been proved, the Coroner remarking that "he thought it would be best not to stamp the family of the deceased with the stigma of insanity". The painful feelings caused in the neighbourhood by the melancholy event turned to sensation when news that James Winch, groom to Mrs Clarke's brother, had hanged himself in an outhouse of his cottage in the village near the church, even while the inquest had been taking place. The inquest on that affair, held at the Coach and Horses, found that James Winch had committed suicide while suffering temporary insanity.

It was Mr Clarke's son, another Thomas Truesdale Clarke (1802-90) who bought Ickenham Manor in 1859 adding it to an already extensive estate, composed of Swakeleys Farm, Tipper Farm, Ivy House Farm and Church Farm, Ryefields, Hercies and Milton Farm. Like his father he was Chairman of the Uxbridge Bench of Magistrates and enjoyed the life of a country gentleman. He planted several coverts and according to his obituary in the local paper, was "the life and soul of many a merry party during the shooting

24. *Some of James Winch's descendants outside their cottage near the churchyard in Ickenham Road. Their home was probably replaced by the pair of cottages now occupied by Ickenham Garden Centre about 1897. Miss Sarah Ann Winch is seated with the children, Charles, Arthur, Louise, William and James Winch, on her left.*

season." He also had a taste for amateur theatricals, which were staged for two days in February each year, the tenants and friends and villagers being invited to watch and entertained with refreshments the first night and the aristocracy of the district, the next. Such people as the Duke of Richmond and the Marchioness of Downshire attended, to the delectation of the populace, who were able to watch the carriages passing.

His son, William Capel Clarke (1832-98), married an heiress Clara Thornhill and added her surname to his own. He mainly lived at his wife's property, Rushton Hall, Northants and Swakeleys was leased to Arthur N. Gilbey, a partner with his brother Walter, in the wine and spirit business. (Gilbey's, a firm centred mainly on Camden Town, was one of the largest distillers of gin in the country.) Arthur Gilbey was keen on croquet and the All England Croquet Championship was played on the lawns at Swakeleys in the 1890s. When Thomas Bryan Clarke-Thornhill put up the estate for auction in 1922, the Gilbeys moved to an estate at Maidenhead.

Humphrey Talbot bought the house and the surrounding land that now forms Swakeleys Park and lived there for a while, until selling it to the Foreign Office Sports Association in 1927. The house was requisitioned during the Second World War and there was a searchlight battery in the grounds. The

25. *Swakeleys Farm on the Harefield side of the River Pinn, opposite Swakeleys, was described as a messuage "at the side of Uxbridge and Northall Commons" in a lease of 1761. The house appeared to be of late seventeenth/early eighteenth century date. After the sale of the Swakeleys estate it survived until about 1958 on the corner of Thornhill Road and Woodstock Drive.*

26. *Ivy House Farm was purchased by the Revd Thomas Clarke before 1780. Alfred Pool, the tenant bought it in 1924 and ran it as a dairy farm.*

27. *Ivy House Farm barn is partially jettied and may have been the original farmhouse, known as Chesiltons or Chisiltons in the seventeenth century. Despite being listed the barn and farm were demolished in 1963, soon after the picture was taken, to make way for Eleanor Grove.*

Foreign Office Sports Association continued to use Swakeleys until 1953. It was purchased by the London Postal Region Sports Club in 1955. By the time the Post Office left in the late 1970s the house was in a state of serious decay. Swakeleys House Ltd formed by three local residents, Keith Chamberlain, Simon Kreiger and Paul Newson, bought it in 1982 and restored all the original features over the next three years. Some new buildings, reasonably in keeping with the outbuildings of the house, were erected in the grounds and the whole is let to Bristol-Myers on a 25-year repairing lease. It is open to the public three days each year.

THE LORDSHIP OF THE MANORS OF ICKENHAM AND SWAKELEYS

The lordship of the manor of Swakeleys was retained by the Lethieulliers in 1750 and passed to the Revd Lascelles Iremonger, son of Benjamin Lethieullier's half brother, after Benjamin's death in 1797. From 1801 it was in the hands of the Newdigates of Harefield. Sir Roger Newdigate's wife, Sophia was great grand daughter of Benjamin Lethieullier's aunt Ann.

The manorial properties were in Uxbridge, Hillingdon End and Cowley. One of them was the tanyard near the Town Mill at the bottom end of Uxbridge High Street.[9]

28. Milton Farm takes its name from the Milton family who were tenants for many years in Victorian times.

Thomas Truesdale Clarke purchased the lordship of the manor of Ickenham, along with Manor Farm in 1859. After the sale of Swakeleys in 1922 the agents retained the lordship until David Pool, the new owner of Manor Farm bought it for £25 in 1927. He died in 1956 and his executors vested the manorial rights in the Borough of Uxbridge.

29. Swakeleys Lodge at the entrance gates in Swakeleys Road. Once two cottages, the property was purchased by the first T.T. Clarke in 1809 and became a gamekeeper's cottage and a lodge.

30. Thomas Truesdale Clarke (1802-90).

The Manors of Harefield

There were three manors in Harefield, the main manor and two submanors, Brackenbury and Moorhall.

THE MANOR OF HAREFIELD

The best known lords of the manor of Harefield were the Newdigates who were in possession by 1446 and still owned land in the area in the 1920s, although a hiatus occurred in the sixteenth and seventeenth centuries. Before the Newdigates came on the scene, Harefield had passed from the Clares (descendants of Richard FitzGilbert) to the Batchworths (Batchworth is in the adjoining parish of Rickmansworth) before 1235 and to the Swanlonds in 1315. Like many Middlesex landowners, the Newdigates were connected with the law. John (d. 1528), a Serjeant-at-Law, produced a large and religiously minded family with his wife Amphilisia Nevill. Their ten sons included two Knights of St John of Jerusalem, who both died at the siege of Rhodes in 1552 and Sebastian, who lived a dashing life as a courtier at Henry VIII's court, before entering the London Charterhouse at Smithfield and becoming one of the Carthusian martyrs in June 1535. Two of the seven daughters became nuns, one with the Dominicans at Dartford and the other was Abbess of Syon.[1]

John Newdigate (1541-92), needing money, exchanged most of his Harefield lands in 1585 with Sir Edmund Anderson who was Chief Justice of the Court of Common Pleas, in return for Arbury, Warwickshire plus a substantial sum. He retained Brackenbury, still an occupied moated site in Breakspear Road South, for his third wife, Winifred and Newdigates continued to be buried in Harefield church. His grandson Richard (1602-78), who was created a Baronet by Charles II despite having been a judge under Oliver Cromwell, (he must have had a subtle legal mind), bought back Harefield in 1675.

During the previous ninety years some interesting Stuart personalities had left their mark upon Harefield. Sir Edmund Anderson sold the estate to trustees for Alice, Dowager Countess of Derby in 1601, as she was about to embark upon an unhappy second marriage with Sir Thomas Egerton, Lord Keeper of the Great Seal and later Lord Chancellor. He had advised her during lawsuits concerning the Earl of Derby's property. His son, later the Earl of Bridgewater, married Alice's second daughter the day following their parents' wedding, both affairs being matters of

31. *The monument of Richard Newdigate (1602-78) in Harefield church. He bought back the manor of Harefield from Sir George Pitt of Stratfield-Saye in 1675. His grandfather had exchanged it for Arbury in Warwickshire and a substantial sum of money ninety years earlier.*

convenience. From her first husband Lady Alice inherited the manor of Colham, of which the neighbouring market town of Uxbridge was a part. Upon her death in January 1637, her grandson William by her eldest daughter, the widowed Lady Chandos, succeeded. He died of smallpox, having languished in gaol for a year awaiting trial for killing a man in a duel, leaving the Harefield property to his wife Jane. She went on to marry Sir William Sedley (brother of the notorious wit, Charles whose scandalous behaviour was noted by Samuel Pepys) and after his death, Sir George Pitt of Stratfield-Saye, from whom Sir Richard Newdigate bought back the manor. Sir Richard's wife was Juliana Leigh, grand-daughter of Sir Thomas Egerton. By another odd connection, Sir Richard's daughter, Frances, secretly married Charles Sedley the wit's bastard son.[2]

32. Dewes Farm as it appeared in 1914. It was known as the Dairy House in 1602 when Queen Elizabeth was received there at the beginning of her wet July visit to the Egertons at Harefield Place.

HAREFIELD PLACE

"A fair house standing on the edge of the hill. The River Colne passing near the same..." Thus John Norden described the old Harefield Place in his *Speculum Britanniae*, published in 1598. The site may be that shown as The Mount on a late-seventeenth century plan. The fish ponds associated with it can be seen today up the path on the north side of the churchyard. Here at the end of July 1602, at the enormous cost of more than £4000, the Egertons entertained the ageing Queen Elizabeth. She was greeted with verses at Dewes Farm, called in those days the Dairy House and conveyed up the Long Walk (thereafter known as the Queen's Walk) and feasted for three days, during which the rain seldom ceased. Apologetic farewells (on account of the weather) finally speeded her on her way. "My only Suyte before you go is that you will pardon the close imprisonment which you have suffered ever since your coming, imputing it not to me but to St Swythen..."

Five or six years later a new house was built lower down the hill, on a level with the church. Little is known of the appearance of this house, the one that Lady Alice lived in, for it was burnt down in 1660 by none other than the elder Sir Charles Sedley who

was reading in bed and presumably knocked over a candle. However the Countess of Derby's (she always used her title from her first marriage) household accounts for 1634-5 reveal a very grand household indeed, with an annual wage bill of £277. The servants included a comptroller, clerk, carter, cook, caterer, footmen, porter, groom, upper maids, wash maids and poultry maids. Lady Alice herself and two grand-daughters and two grandsons made up the family. They were Alice and Elizabeth Hastings, daughter of Lady Alice's second daughter, Elizabeth and George and William, sons of her eldest daughter, Lady Chandos. Lady Chandos had entered into an unfortunate second marriage with the homosexual Lord Castlehaven, whose son, James, had been allied with her 12-year-old daughter, Elizabeth. The girl was corrupted by her father-in-law and his servants (acting under his directions) and never recovered, becoming estranged from her family and apparently leading a questionable life, for in 1655 she and a friend were taken by the constable in the common garden and lodged all night in the cage. Lord Castlehaven was tried by his peers for a rape against his own wife and sodomy and was beheaded in 1631. During the trial Lady Castlehaven, who not surprisingly reverted to her former name of Chandos, stayed

33. *Lord Castlehaven, second husband of Lady Alice's daughter, Lady Chandos. Lady Alice, noting his vicious character and fearing that he would seize her goods at her death, built Haydon Hall in the neighbouring parish of Ruislip, "to have a place to lay my stuffe in out of my Lord Castlehaven's fingering". In the event he was executed in 1631 and she survived him by six years.*

at Harefield with her other children. The boys remained with their grandmother.

Food for the household was purchased by the caterer, regularly from Uxbridge and about twice a month from London, whence such goods as soap and wine were brought back, sometimes by the carter and sometimes by the Uxbridge wagoner. Lady Alice was the great lady of the neighbourhood and when she travelled to West Drayton to visit Lady Paget, the bells were rung in Uxbridge. She gave five shillings to the ringers. A large party gathered in July 1634 with her son-in-law, the Earl of Bridgewater bringing his own cook and his trumpeters. The next month it was Lord Coleraine and Lord Manchester who brought their cooks and three more, one from London, were hired to help in the kitchens. Her grandson Lord Chandos married Lord Manchester's daughter as his first wife and the arrangements may have been discussed during these lavish festivities.[3]

Lady Alice and Sir Thomas Egerton had enlarged the park and kept a herd of deer. The keeper's lodge later became Park Lodge Farm after the deer had gone. The present farmhouse is a rebuild of nineteenth century date.

AFTER THE FIRE

Two lodges and various offices was all that was left of the manor house when Sir Richard Newdigate (1602-78) bought it back. His widow occupied one of these remnants until her death in 1685 and Lady Long who kept a pair of pet deer, lived in the other. In March 1693 the principal tenants of Harefield manor swore: "That the site of the manor house is yet very apparent south-east of the church, but the house has been burnt down some years and there is nothing now but two lodges and the old offices remaining and the foundations of the old house, viz: The front is now very plain to be seen being 137 foot long and the back part foundations, the foundation the Fountain Garden wall is built upon and the north-east end, come within 12 foot of the great fir tree."[4]

A new hall with Dutch gables, perhaps built by Sir Richard Newdigate (1644-1710), joined the two lodges in the eighteenth century and is shown in a line drawing in Daniel Lyson's account of Middlesex parishes. Sir Richard, who became mentally unhinged in later life, had produced plans for a grandiose house with columns at the front in 1699, but they came to nothing as he was engaged in lawsuits with his family. The site of Harefield Place is now occupied by the Australian Military Cemetery. The warmly coloured brick walls that surrounded one of the gardens are still to be seen, with a coach house of mainly later brick in one corner.

A MODERN VILLA

Sir Roger Newdigate (1719-1806), the 5th and last Baronet, who lived mainly at Arbury and stayed in London during parliamentary terms, conveyed Harefield Place and a number of nearby farms to John Truesdale of St James's, Westminster in 1761, leaving himself with no great house in Harefield. On his visits he made use of Brackenbury, but by 1786, either because he felt the inconvenience or had some cash to spare, he started work on a new 'villa' in Pinnox Wood on the wasteland in the extreme south-west of the parish. Henry Couchman was the architect. He had already 'gothicised' Arbury for Sir Roger, but employed a plain style in Harefield. Sir Roger noted in his diary for the 11th April 1786:

"Leaden plate laid in foundation of Harefield Lodge..."

Harefield Lodge remained the name of the villa until about 1818. Harefield Place by the church had passed to Sir William Baynes in 1780. His son Sir Christopher Baynes appears to have demolished it and thrown the land into that of New Inn Farm, standing on the roadside in front of the church. When Jane Parker, widow of Sir Roger's cousin's son, purchased Harefield Place in 1812 all the buildings were described as "all now abated".[5] The name was transferred to Harefield Lodge and the present Harefield

34. *Harefield Place at the end of the eighteenth century. St Mary's church can be seen on the left. The hall stands on the site of the Australian Military Cemetery.*

Place, now superior offices overlooking the A40, is Sir Roger's new villa of 1786.

Sir Roger was childless and what was left of the manorial estate, (he had sold a lot in 1752 to another landed family, the Cookes of Harefield Park), passed to the descendants of his female cousin, Millicent, who had married William Parker. Jane Parker's grandson Charles, who had adopted the surname Newdigate-Newdegate, sold a large portion of his lands including the house, to Henry Richard Cox of Hillingdon House in 1877. The remaining Newdigate estate was dispersed by Sir Francis Alexander Newdigate-Newdegate in the 1920s and 30s.

BRACKENBURY

Thomas Brackenburgh who made his will in March 1391, naming his wife and her son Thomas Brakynbury as executors, owned the estate called Brackenbury towards the south end of Breakspear Road South. It was a manor, but subordinate to that of Harefield. The moat probably dates from the fourteenth century, but the house standing today is of two periods, sixteenth century and seventeenth century. By the 1550s Brackenbury was part of the Newdigates' demesne and let to "My Lord Chamberlayn" at 100 shillings a year. Apparently there was a fire in the early 1560s and Lord Hastings, the Lord Chamberlain agreed to rebuild the house as it stood previously, or better.

This is the house granted to Winifred Newdigate for life at the time of the sale to Sir Edmund Anderson and retained by the family. It was a superior house, leased to aristocrats or London merchants, well furnished as an inventory taken in 1605 testifies.[6] A well-paved and wainscoted hall with screen and fixed benches had several tables and forms. It was well glazed and heated by a fire with a chimney. The buttery also had a chimney. A parlour had been "used as a chapell in Lord Loughborough his tyme" (Lord Hastings of Loughborough). The kitchen had a range. There was "a pretty convenient gallery matted with the windows and glass thereof in some dekay" above the great chamber, as well as "a fyne lytell gallery. All in good repayre saving a little plaistering of the watles and that the windoes of that lytle gallery doo want glasse are somewhat dekayed." At least eight bedchambers are recorded, one with its own house of office (loo). Outside stood a gate house, dovecote, brewhouse, stables and barns. It sounds altogether too grand for Ralph Wingfield, the farm bailiff who lived there in the mid-seventeenth century, but it may have been past its best, as most of it was replaced about 1685 by the splendid seventeenth-century main house that stands today.

The Newdigates' steward let Brackenbury to farmers, who were not always successful. John Wise agreed to take it from Ladyday 1765 for seven years,

35. The coachhouse of Harefield Place in the early twentieth century with the garden wall on the left. It had been converted into a cottage and still survives as part of the Nursery Garden that now occupies the old walled garden.

36. The new Harefield Place built in Pinnox Wood at the southern end of the parish in 1786 by Sir Roger Newdigate. The architect was Henry Couchman.

37. Brackenbury manor house stands within a moated site on Breakspear Road. The portion on the left dates from Lord Hastings' rebuilding after a fire in the 1560s. The main part of the house was erected c.1685.

the lease specifying that Sir Roger should have the use of the kitchen, two bedchambers and garrets over them, a lock-up bedchamber, a cellar and stabling for horses "when required".[7] John was to pay £126 per annum for 112 acres and was allowed to keep the muck. He had to lay two loads of dung for every load of hay carried off to keep the land in good heart. On Thursday 16th February 1769 (about five weeks before his rent was due) he ran away with one of the horses and two men came with a cart about

midnight and took away "the best part of his goods, his two best cows, the other horse and his wife". They paid the maid her wages and on taking leave of the girl said "she would never see them more". A sad little story.

Brackenbury continued to be let as a farm after the sale to Henry Richard Cox in 1877 until much of the Cox estate was conveyed to the Cavendish Land Company in 1918 and Brackenbury was immediately sold to James Guthrie Reid, whose widow, Dame Clarissa Guthrie Reid lived there until her death in 1931. It had become a gentleman's residence and was described in that year as an "early English residence" with old world gardens and picturesque farm buildings and had a tennis court.

COPTHALL FARM

The Brackenbury estate included the nearby Copthall Farm, a timber-framed building with a later brick facade, dating in part from the sixteenth century when it was referred to as Auditors in manorial rentals. Richard Warde was tenant in 1559. The Guthrie Reids owned it along with Brackenbury and Dame Clarissa's executors sold it to Frank Dalton who was already the tenant in 1933. The Dalton family operate Copthall Farm in 1995.

38. Copthall Farm in Breakspear Road was part of the Brackenbury estate. It was known as Auditors in the early sixteenth century. The Treadaway family were farmers here in Victorian times. The present farmers, the Daltons, have owned it since 1933.

39. Pynchester moat was part of Brackenbury. Remains of flint walls, pottery and a key-hole shaped oven suggest that a house stood on the site in the fourteenth and fifteenth century.

PYNCHESTER

Across Breakspear Road South on the bank of the River Pinn, the moated site called Pynchester was also part of Brackenbury. Flint walls, a key-hole shaped oven and 'curing chamber' and pottery dating from the fourteenth or fifteenth century were uncovered by excavations in the centre of the site by the Uxbridge Archaeological Group in 1966-9. The moat is in a bend of the River Pinn and fed by a channel from the river. The estate extended over the stream at that point to include a field called Ickenham Redding in Ickenham parish.

MOORHALL

The Knights Hospitallers of St John of Jerusalem were first given land in Harefield in the 1180s by Beatrice de Bollers and her son Geoffrey, members of the Clare family together with the advowson (the right to appoint incumbents) of Harefield church. Other grants, one of Bayhurst Wood, followed over the next hundred years and a cell was established on the moors, south-west of the church. The estate was known as the manor of Moorhall and four messuages and cottages: Crows Nest, Maud Field, Weybeards and Wilkins, were said to be held of Moorhall in the late sixteenth century.[8] The Knights lost the property at the Reformation and Henry VIII granted it to Robert Tyrwhit in 1542, with permission to sell to John Newdigate, after which time Moorhall was a sub-manor of Harefield. Thereafter it was leased as a substantial farm. Richard Bugberd was paying 75 shillings for the site of the manor and demesne in 1558.

A timber-framed house and a flint barn of great age stood at Moorhall within living memory. The barn was believed to date from the early thirteenth century and was probably the hall of the Knights, degenerating into a barn after Moorhall became a farm. The house had massive timbers and had begun life as a hall house in the fourteenth century. Many later additions, including a brick façade and inserted chimneys, effectively disguised its origins. The house was burnt down in 1922 and the barn and 33 acres

40. Moorhall as depicted by Lysons. The flint barn on the left may have been a chapel in the time of the Knights Hospitallers. The timber-framed hall dated from the fourteenth century, but was unfortunately burnt down in 1922.

*41. The Bishop of Kensington and the Revd H.S. Cochran at the reopening and dedication of Moorhall in September 1927.
Two Knights of St John, Mr Pirie Gordon of* The Times *and Mr Fincham are in the centre, led by a churchwarden and the
secretary of the church council.*

*42. The early thirteenth-century flint barn shown in
Illustration 40 presented a sorry appearance in the 1920s.
Gypsies appear to have moved in.*

were sold by Sir Francis Newdigate to Uxbridge
Rural District Council in 1926. The vicar, the Revd
H. Cochran leased it in 1927 and put it into repair
for use as a Sunday School and Mission Hall. After
the Second World War the building degenerated into
a football changing room and by 1953 the roof had
fallen in. Great efforts were exerted to have what
was the oldest building in the parish, with the exception of the church, restored, but it was scandal-
ously demolished in 1961 in the teeth of local opposition.

43. St Giles's church in 1795, showing William Say's double gabled aisle from the outside.

St Giles's Church, Ickenham

THE BUILDING

St Giles is one of a group of small Middlesex parish churches, similar in size and style to St Mary's Northolt and St Mary's, Norwood. Just when a church was built in Ickenham is unclear. There was no mention of a priest in the Domesday Survey and a manuscript at St Paul's Cathedral naming Reyold Cabus as patron of the living in the mid-thirteenth century is the earliest reference to a parish. The nave and chancel of the present church both date from the second half of the fourteenth century, and could have been built during the rectorship of John de Brokhampton between 1353-1382. A timbered bell turret was added to the nave in the fifteenth century.

A brick-built aisle was erected on the north side of the nave in 1575 at the instigation of William Say. He was Proctor of the the ecclesiastical Court of Arches, and had lived in Ickenham, possibly at Buntings next to the church, with his wife Isabel from the 1530s, producing sixteen children. She was the daughter of Thomas Nelham of Ruislip. Perhaps more accommodation was necessary in the church for his family, some of whom stayed in Ickenham after their own marriages. Although he paid for the building of the aisle, William Say stated in his will that the parishioners of Ickenham were in his debt for the charge of making the bricks, and continues "I am content...and in consideration that I have my pews there for me and my house which pews I made with all their consents at myne owne charge. And for that I do intend to be buried in the same Chappel to let that debt be remit in such burials as should happen to be made there out of my dwelling house after the rate of three shillings and fourpence for every corps."[1] The south porch is of similar date. These are rare examples of Elizabethan work in a Middlesex church.

A further addition to the nave, also in brick, was built by Sir John Harrington of Swakeleys in the mid-seventeenth century, to be a mortuary chapel. It was used for burials from Swakeleys until 1892. Tall niches around the walls held upended coffins and were perhaps sealed, as the inscription recording the death of Sir Edward Harrington, father of Sir John, in 1652, starts "Within this arch is immured.....". Other plates relating to Sir John's daughters say "Within this pillar is inshrined..." and "Within this place is inceosed [sic]...." Later bodies were piled

44. *St Giles's church and village pump c.1900*

on the floor. The chapel was cleared in 1914, when thirty coffins were removed and reinterred in the graveyard. The chapel is now dedicated to St John and houses the Jacobean altar originally in the church proper.

Spurling in his *Church Walks Around Middlesex* was appalled at the state of St Giles in the 1840s. Work was undertaken in the 1870s, when an arcade between the nave and north aisle was restored and a chancel arch (a sad lack in Spurling's view) was inserted.

The nave was extended westwards in 1958 to provide more accommodation for the expanding parish, but fits in well with the medieval structure as the windows were copied from the fourteenth-century ones elsewhere in the church and old timbers were brought in to form the roof trusses.

The saddest monument in the church is the marble effigy of Sir Robert Clayton's son, who was born and died at Swakeleys on an August day in 1665. It was dug up from the churchyard in 1921 and now rests on a window sill in the chancel. The baby appears again, as a rather older child, on his parents' monument at Bletchingly, Surrey.

45. *The fourteenth-century nave and chancel at St Giles. The arcade was restored and the chancel arch was built in the 1870s. The aisle of 1575 can be glimpsed through the arcade arches.*

46. *The Jacobean font in St Giles. It was used as a tea caddy, or more likely a work table, at Swakeleys for many years, and was returned to the church by Miss Helen Cochrane, granddaughter of Thomas Truesdale Clarke, c.1921.*

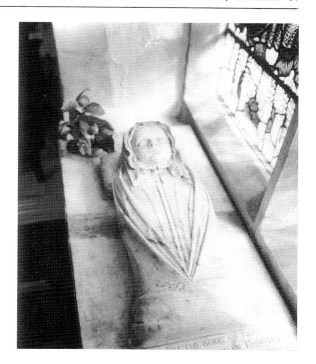

47. (Above) The present St John's Chapel was probably built by Sir John Harrington of Swakeleys between 1640-50. Coffins used to stand in the tall niches and others were piled on the floor. They were taken out and reinterred in the churchyard in 1914. The altar and houseling benches are Jacobean and came from the main body of the church.

48. (Below) The nave was extended westwards in 1958, but blends well with the ancient walls, as the windows were copied from the fourteenth-century ones elsewhere in the church.

49. (Top right) A poignant monument to the only son of Sir Robert Clayton and his wife, Dame Mary. The child was born and died on 16th August 1665, while his parents were living at Swakeleys. He appears again, as an older child, on his parents' monument in Bletchingly church, Surrey.

THE GLEBE AND PARSONAGE

John Cabus sold the advowson – the right to nominate the incumbent – of St Giles to Laurance del Brok in 1257 and thereafter it passed with the lordship of the manor to the Shorediches until 1743, when it was sold to Thomas Clarke of Spring Gardens, Westminster. He put his own son, the Revd Thomas Clarke, into the living in 1747. The patronage stayed with the Clarkes until Thomas Bryan Clarke-Thornhill transferred it to Eton College in 1923.

The extent of the parish at the outset is difficult to determine. As suggested in Chapter 1, Brackenbury could have been in Ickenham rather than Harefield in the fourteenth century. Colour is lent to this view by the fact that Lord Hastings who lived at Brackenbury had a daughter, Kateryn, christened at St Giles in August 1542 with two royal godmothers, Queen Kateryn (Catherine Parr), whose sister Mr Harbord's wife stood proxy, and Lady Margaret Angles, the king's niece.

The appointed incumbents were rectors, not vicars, and therefore had the right to collect all the tithes in the parish. The Bishop of Worcester who was rector of Hillingdon sued John Spygurnell in 1453 for collecting tithes on lands called Tykenham, which for some years before had been considered to be in Ickenham, but were then pronounced to be in Hillingdon. The fields named Swillington, Down Barns Field etc were later definitely in Ickenham.[2] Obviously confusion reigned over the parish boundaries after so much movement and division in the medieval period.

According to an account of 1649, the rector's glebe land was scattered throughout the common fields of Ickenham, but amounted to rather less than 15 acres, with two portions of meadow in addition. A moated rectory was built well away from the church close to the common fields. It was down the lane that is called Glebe Avenue today. Clovelly Avenue is now on the site. A map of 1664 shows the house with a dovecote and 14½ acres of enclosed land around it, mostly in Little Horsecroft and Great Horsecroft. The meadow in the mid-18th century was at Beatonswood at the far end of Ickenham Green and Chestlands, which was a detached piece of Ickenham lying within Hillingdon parish, near the present Hillingdon Station. The enclosure of the common fields and waste in 1781 greatly enhanced the benefice. The rector (Thomas Clarke at the time) received 248 acres in compensation for his common field glebe and the tithes that were suppressed on newly enclosed land and on some of the old enclosures.

50. Glebe Farm, Ickenham, was the rectory until 1750. It stood within a moat on the edge of the common fields. Clovelly Avenue is now on the site. The house appears to have been given a new front in the eighteenth century. The Woodland family were farmers here in Victorian times and two of them are pictured below.

When the Revd Thomas Clarke moved to Swakeleys shortly after his marriage in 1750, the parsonage and glebe was let out to farm. The Revd Thomas Bracken who came to the parish in 1800 found the old parsonage house unsatisfactory, being "an ancient wooden building, consisting only of four rooms" too small and mean for his habitation and inconveniently situated half a mile from the parish church and that part of the parish in which the parishioners resided. He probably wanted to be nearer to Swakeleys and Buntings, where congenial company might be found. Thomas Truesdale Clarke let him have three closes, Orchard Close, Butcher's Field and Betty Marlow's Field in Swakeleys Road (then called Back Lane), to erect a parsonage house "for the further improvement and better accommodation of present and future incumbents and the parishioners at large, by promoting the residence of the Rector amongst them."[3] An imposing classical edifice in keeping with Thomas Bracken's view of his status was erected, but whether he always resided there is uncertain. He died in 1815 at Kensington Square at the age of 48. The Revd D.W.W. Carmichael, the last of the incumbents to be presented by the Clarke-Thornhills, perhaps found it too grand and moved to a more modest, new rectory built in a corner of the grounds on Swakeleys Road in 1927. Ickenham Girls' High School moved into the old rectory. It was demolished about 1961 and Rectory Way now stands on the site.

The old house survived as Glebe Farm until being demolished to make way for suburban development in the 1930s. A photograph taken early this century of two members of the Woodland family who farmed there for several generations, shows a Georgian-fronted house, probably a brick façade added to a timber-framed building. It looks much bigger than Mr Bracken suggested in 1800. The moat was only partly in evidence in the seventeenth century and has since completely disappeared.

RECTORS

The Visitation of the clergy in 1586 found Henry Kendall to be simple, which sounds rather worrying as he had already been in office since 1568 and apparently remained until 1624! Maybe he was just not learned and lived a simple country life farming his glebe. Robert Say who followed him, possibly a grandson of William Say, was certainly educated, graduating from New College, Oxford in 1599 and a Doctor of Divinity by 1614, but he stayed only for one year. Only once do the Shorediches seem to have given the living to one of their own family. The Revd John Shorediche (1662-1724) was put in by his father Col. Richard Shorediche in 1714. He was a pluralist of a sort being vicar of Ruislip at the same time.

51. Ickenham Rectory 1800-1927. The Revd Thomas Bracken's new rectory was built on Betty Marlow's Field in Swakeleys Road (then Back Lane) It subsequently became Ickenham Girls' High School and was demolished in 1961. Rectory Way is now on the site of the house and grounds.

52. Harefield church from the south-east in 1794, showing the Brackenbury Chapel before it was extended to form a south aisle.

St Mary's, Harefield

THE BUILDING

The glory of St Mary's is its monuments, particularly those dating from the seventeenth and eighteenth centuries, many decorated with colourful heraldic devices. The most magnificent is that to Lady Alice, Dowager Countess of Derby in the south-east corner of the chancel. Her figure, dressed in a red farthingale and ermine trimmed cloak, with long unbound hair and a coronet on the head, lies on a Venetian style bed. Curtains falling from a domed canopy, are drawn back and tied around the black marble bed posts. Her three daughters, similarly dressed to herself, kneel in niches below and the whole is adorned with her heraldic achievements. Maximilian Colt designed this delectable memorial and perhaps did better for Lady Alice in Harefield than he did for Queen Elizabeth in Westminster Abbey. She does rather dominate the church, however, because the bed encroaches upon the altar and the chancel is in any case set high above the nave, up five steps.

Part of the west wall of the nave dates from the twelfth century. The church then was probably a simple nave and chancel. A north chapel was added in the thirteenth century and the chancel was rebuilt. The chapel is raised to the same height as the chancel and became the Breakspear Chapel, where the Ashbys of Breakspear House have their tombs. It is now the Australian chapel. An external door, now stopped up, once gave the family private access. Near the door on the outside wall hang two unusual memorials, being dedicated to servants of the Ashby family. That to Robert Mossendew, William Ashby's gamekeeper, shows him with his gun, game bag and spaniel, Tray and has a long poetic inscription, comparing his faithfulness to that of the dog.

When the nave was rebuilt in the fourteenth century, another chapel was added at the south-east end, known as the Brackenbury Chapel. Perhaps it was originally dedicated to St Thomas and is where Thomas Brackenburgh wanted to be buried. According to his will of 1391 he left two shillings for its mending. The outside wall has an attractive chequerboard pattern of dressed limestone and flint, which was continued along the new wall, when the chapel was extended in 1841 to form a south aisle. The old south porch was destroyed at that time. Although bequests were made towards the building of the

53. *Lady Alice, Dowager Countess of Derby lies on her Venetian style bed beside the altar, with her three daughters mourning her in the niches below. The heraldic eagles at the corners of the tester allude to her position as Lady of Man, during her first marriage, as the Stanleys were lords of the Isle of Man.*

54. *The Mossendew Memorial on the ouside wall of the Breakspear Chapel is carved in wood with a painted inscription. It was restored and rededicated in memory of Elona Cuthbertson, local historian, who was organising the work at the time of her death in 1992.*

north aisle in 1500 and a steeple in 1545, no pictures exist showing a steeple on top of the tower.

A major restoration of the chancel was undertaken in 1768, under the direction of the architect, Henry Keene. New oak stalls were built, though the old wainscoting was fastened against the wall, some monuments were refixed and perhaps rearranged, the window on the side of the chancel was stopped up, the chancel arch was raised and the mason was "to clear up altar window and make good ditto for new glazing". The three-decker pulpit and box pews are eighteenth century and quaint reminders of the more feudal past. According to a seating plan of 1803, the servants at Breakspears sat in the pew below their master's chapel and a special pew was always "appropriated to women churching".

A PECULIAR JURISDICTION

Beatrice de Bollers and her son Geoffrey granted the advowson of the church to the Knights Hospitallers of St John of Jerusalem between 1180-1185. The Bishop of London, Gilbert Foliot, established Harefield as a 'peculiar jurisdiction' – a parish exempt from the jurisdiction of the bishop in whose diocese it lay.[1] This freedom was contested from time to time after the Reformation, when the Newdigates were patrons, but the situation was considered lawful and continued until 1847, when all peculiars were transferred to bishops. Because of this anomaly the clergy of Harefield were styled variously as chaplain, curate, perpetual vicar and minister. Only in 1870 was the parish given the status of a vicarage. The Newdigates continued as patrons and Viscount Daventry, a descendant, assisted in the finding of a new vicar for Harefield in 1995.

55. St Mary's before the First World War. The Breakspear chapel can be seen on the left of the porch. The south aisle built in 1841 is on the right.

INCUMBENTS AND THEIR MAINTENANCE

The Knights Hospitaller were obliged to find and provide maintenance for a chaplain to serve Harefield church, but as rectors they were entitled to collect the tithes for themselves. The tithes and patronage went with the lordship of the manor in the ninety years that the Newdigates were away from Harefield and should have been bought back by Sir Richard Newdigate along with the manor in 1675, but George Pitt, sold them to higher bidders, resulting in several landowners owning the tithes on their own estates. This meant that the poor incumbent had no income from tithes, nor glebe land (that held held by the priest of 1086 having been incorporated with Moorhall in medieval times). Neither was there a priest's house. The pre-Reformation priests perhaps lodged at Moorhall. From the sixteenth century an annual salary was paid; it was £6 13s 4d in 1547, but where the parson lived is unclear. It would have been convenient for the clergyman to combine the care of the parish with the position of private chaplain at Harefield Place and John Pritchett seems to have done so in Lady Alice's time. Later he purchased a house of his own called Rythes, forerunner of Harefield Park, now Harefield Hospital. His successor John Conant was Lord Chandos's chaplain during the Civil War and kept that place, after being supplanted at the church by Mr Hoare who was a Parliament man.

Two rooms at the Almshouses built under the terms of Lady Alice's will, were set aside for the use of the curate, along with £25 a year charged on the manorial estate. He was to be available to read prayers for the almswomen. The Newdigates continued to pay the salary, increasing it occasionally, into the twentieth century, assisted latterly by the Ecclesiastical Commissioners. The rather niggardly sum proved insufficient and rooms at the Almshouses too confined for family men. (Two more rooms were added in 1745 to ease matters.) The Revd John Baldwin who died in 1674, lived at Eversden down by the river, where his widow, Dorothy was still to be found, living with her tenant and his family in 1699 when Gregory King made his survey of Harefield. The house is still there, but has been renamed Black Jack's Cottage.

56. Eversden down by the Colne (now beside the canal and named Black Jack's Cottage) where the Revd John Baldwin lived in the 1670s.

57. John Pritchett has a handsome monument in the church, surmounted by the arms of his bishopric.

JOHN PRITCHETT, BISHOP OF GLOUCESTER

John Pritchett (household chaplain to Lady Alice in the 1630s and chaplain at Harefield with breaks from the 1630s to 1672) was a pluralist and indulged in nepotism as well.[2] He was a royalist, "loyal to church and king and was driven from office" during and after the Civil War, but reaped a rich reward after the Restoration, becoming rector of St Andrew Undershaft and Harlington, vicar of St Giles Cripplegate and prebend of Mora. He partly lived at Rythes throughout and seems to have served Harefield church again for a time at least, before ending his career as Bishop of Gloucester from 1672-1680. He secured the post of Receiver for Gloucester for his son and that of Principal Registrar of the Bishop's Consistory Court for his son-in-law, John Stanyon. The Stanyons were already living in Harefield and moved into Rythes after the Bishop's death. The work in Gloucester was undertaken by a deputy who received a quarter of the profits, sending the rest on to Mr Stanyon. Incidentally John Stanyon lost his position as Keeper of the East India Company's Pepper Warehouse, under a cloud, because he had been involved in private trade.

58. *The Johnson family outside their home, the former coach house of Harefield Place. In 1909 Mrs Johnson was described as the 'sextoness' in an article in the* Home Counties Magazine. *Her daughter, Connie, seen sitting on her lap, grew up to be verger of the church and a very well-known figure in Harefield.*

ROGER DAVIES AND CLANDESTINE MARRIAGES[3]

Mr Roger Davies came to Harefield in the 1670s and was installed by George Pitt, a year or two before Sir Richard Newdigate returned as patron of the living. An expanding family drove him to take the job of Lecturer at Watford, where there was a house, whence he rode over to Harefield to take prayers on Sundays and Wednesdays. His only duty at Watford was to preach a sermon each Tuesday before the market opened. He became involved in a dispute with Richard Priest, parish clerk and sexton, over the conduct of marriages at Harefield. St Mary's was a popular venue for weddings because it was a peculiar and anyone could marry there with neither banns nor bishop's licence. While Mr Davies was absent in Watford, the clerk had been busy arranging for couples (many of them no doubt runaways or under age) to be married in the church by clergymen from nearby parishes, his own fee being five shillings per wedding. When the minister found out he seized the church keys and registers, effectively shutting out the clerk. The villagers sided with Richard Priest and wrote to Sir Richard Newdigate at Arbury in December 1679, asking him to arbitrate.

Thus began an affair which at times descended into farce, involving the Bishop of London in support of Mr Davies and Judge Jeffreys as head of the Commissioners for Ecclesiastical Affairs. It continued with the Bishop challenging the status of Harefield as a peculiar jurisdiction, but ended with the Newdigates establishing their independence once and for all in 1699. The farcical element was introduced early on, when Sir Richard brought another minister to Harefield on a Sunday morning in 1679 and had his butler and coachman from the Place hide in the pulpit and reading desk, armed with feather dusters, to prevent Mr Davies' entrance!

Rules governing church attendance laid down at the manor court in 1692, probably arose from this affair: "All persons or householders or inhabitants within the parish of Harefield who are not dissenters from the Church of England doe once a fortnight go to Church on the Sabbath Day and stay there during the time of Divine Service and sermon (if there be any sermon there)." Children were not to play in the street during service time. Those over eight and servants were to be sent to church by their parents or masters and mistresses. Married people were to take turns in attending church so that one could stay at home to look after younger children.[4]

59. Harefield Vicarage, built in the 1850s during the incumbency of the Revd John Lightfoot and used by the clergy until 1927. The attractive Victorian-Tudor style building survived until the 1950s, when it was replaced by a block of flats, Harland Lodge, commemorating the name of Harefield's longest-serving vicar.

60. *Harefield High Street in the early years of this century with the carriage drive of the vicarage (now Merle Avenue) on the right. The building in the centre of the picture is the King's Head (recently renamed Disraeli's).*

61. Revd Albert Augustus Harland, vicar of Harefield 1870-1920.

THE PARSONAGE

Less turbulent characters ministered at Harefield during the following centuries. Some of them must have been quite prosperous. Edward Barnard, minister from 1803-1808, could afford to live at Harefield Grove. John Penrose only ran the church for five years from 1809-14, but his name is remembered today because of the school that is named after him. The Revd William Henry Rowlatt (1775-1863) leased Whiteheath Farm in 1810 and only took Holy Orders in 1814, after his father had lost his money. He left both the farm and the parish after only four years, and sadly his twin daughters, Fanny and Julia, were also left behind, buried in the churchyard.

At last in 1852 a rather grand parsonage was built for John Lightfoot who served the parish from 1825-64. The house stood near the top of the hill away from the church, on the opposite side of the High Street to Harefield House, in grounds of 8½ acres. Three more clergymen lived there, Revd R.C.W. Collins (1864-70), Revd Albert Augustus Harland

62. *Cumberland House, which became the vicarage in 1927.*

(1870-1920) and Revd H.S. Cochran (1920-7). When Mr Cochran retired the house was sold and the grounds were divided into building plots. One plot was purchased in 1929 to be the site of a future Roman Catholic church (built in 1963) and the rest of the estate came into the possession of James Whittle, the Northwood builder, while Mr Dudley Hill and Miss Roberts leased the house and gardens. Mr Whittle's executors auctioned the land in 1946 and Merle Avenue was built over the next few years. A block of flats called Harland Lodge occupies the site of the vicarage.

63. *An early view of the Australian cemetery, when some of the graves were marked by simple wooden crosses and the official headstones were facing east. Nowadays they face west.*

A spacious house called Cumberland House, built by the Collets as a family house, was purchased and remained in use by the Revd D.G.A. Connor until his retirement in 1995. That, in its turn is shortly to be redeveloped.

AUSTRALIAN MILITARY CEMETERY AND THE ANZAC DAY CEREMONY

Harefield Park was used as an Australian Military Hospital during the First World War and those who died were buried with full military honours at St Mary's. The portion of the graveyard where Harefield Place had once stood was consecrated as a Military Cemetery and is reached today through a memorial gateway. The village school lent a Union flag to drape over the coffins, which after the war was given by the headmaster, E.C. Jeffery, to the last commanding officer of the hospital for the children of Australia. It was placed in Adelaide High School and Harefield school received a new Union flag and an Australian flag. The school children have been making a pilgrimage to the cemetery each Anzac Day since 1921 to place flowers on the 112 graves (111 soldiers of the Australian Army and one Nursing Sister) and the Australian flag is flown. Sir Francis Newdigate-Newdegate, who had been Governor-general of Tasmania and Queensland, together with Mr Billyard-Leake, owner of Harefield Park gave the obelisk in 1921 and the entrance archway and gate were erected in 1924.

Men with distinguished military careers lie in the other part of the graveyard. General Gerald Goodlake won a VC in the Crimean War and Sergeant Robert Ryder was awarded one in the First World War.

64. This Edwardian view of Breakspears shows the house from the south-west. Captain Tarleton added the bay-windowed library on the right in 1897 and the service end on the left, hidden by the tree. The central section dates from the seventeenth century, although the Venetian window was probably inserted about 1740.

Breakspears

BREAKSPEARS AND THE ASHBYS

Members of the Breakspear family lived in Harefield at the end of the fourteenth century and gave their name to two houses; one, later known as Breakspear-by-the-heath or Little Breakspears, stood between the heath and the Further Park (now Old Park Wood) and was demolished in the 1930s; the other, the mansion called Breakspears which now stands empty in Breakspear Road. About 1440, the Breakspears fade from Harefield documents and shortly after-wards George Ashby's name appears and his de-scendants lived at Breakspears for the next 400 years. He was a courtier, being Clerk of the Signet (private secretary) to Henry VI's queen, Margaret of Anjou.[1] He died in 1474 and he and his wife Margaret are commemorated in a small non-pictorial brass in the Breakspear Chapel at St Mary's. His grandson, George (d.1515) served both Henry VII and Henry VIII as Clerk of the Signet, while his great grandson, Thomas was Clerk of the Spicery to Queen Elizabeth, shortly before his death in 1559. Thereafter the courtly connection seems to come to an end, but Thomas's grandson, Robert (1563-1618) was a knight and Robert's son Francis was created a baronet in 1623 shortly before he died. Some of the Ashbys had catholic sympathies – Sir Robert was fined in 1604 for hiding Jesuit priests.[2]

The Breakspear estate at the end of the sixteenth century, stretched along Breakspear Road, including Gauntletts, the large field between the house and Bayhurst Wood, Kitchen Fields, Langley Farm and land called Lyttons and Shepherds that is now the Model Dairy Farm, and included Battleswells (or Battlerswells) on the road to Batchworth Heath. Francis Ashby (1592-1623) left a very young daugh-ter, Alice, born 1620, as his sole heir. She married Alexander Lynde (or Lyne) of Rickmansworth as soon as she was old enough (about 15), and her mother married Beverley Britten at about the same time. The Lyndes sold off much of the property, and as Alice seems to have left no children, her cousin Robert Ashby (1627-74) eventually succeeded to the depleted estate.

The Ashbys, although prolific, suffered a great many early deaths, particularly among the boys, from the late seventeenth century onwards, so that when a later Robert Ashby died in 1769, he was survived by his daughter, Elizabeth and no male

65. *Langley Farm viewed from one of the fields called Kitchen Fields.*

66. *Bourne Farm at the foot of Drake's Hill takes its name from the stream or bourne that runs under the road behind the white rails. Bournes was first mentioned in 1428 and was sometimes known as Hamonds in the sixteenth century. The house shown in the photograph was bombed in 1944, but rebuilt in exactly the same style. This hilly portion of Breakspear Road was called Drake's Hill from the time that the Wickham-Drakes lived at Breakspears.*

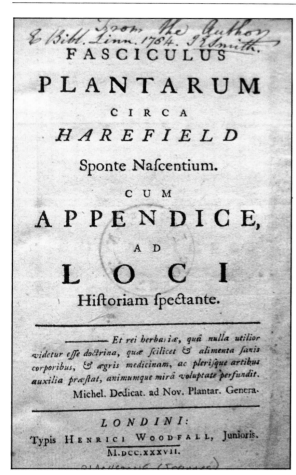

68. The dovecot at Breakspears was mentioned in a survey of 1640. In 1995 it only just survives in an appalling condition. It used to be the job of the estate carpenter to climb the stairs weekly, to wind the clock in the cupola.

67. The frontispiece of John Blackstone's book about plants growing around Harefield. It was published in 1737. This copy was presented to Linnaeus by the author and was given to the Linnaean Society, along with many other books and papers belonging to Linnaeus, by J.E. Smith.

Ashbys at all. Elizabeth married a Westminster apothecary called John Joseph Partridge a year later, this not being the first time that an apothecary had joined the family. Elizabeth's aunt, Sarah, had married Edward Blackstone, an apothecary's son and their eldest child John Blackstone (1711-53) had become an apothecary and well-known herbalist who wrote two books, one of them being *Fasciculus plantarum circa Harefield sponte nascentium* (A little bundle of plants growing around Harefield), published in 1737. Blackstone's mother, Sarah, left him part of Maud Fields alongside Bayhurst Wood, where he had already noted that the snake's head fritillary grew, the earliest reference to this attractive flower in the British Isles.

Elizabeth Partridge's only son, Joseph Ashby Partridge, having no children, left his estates, now built up again, to William Wickham-Drake, a relative of his wife, in 1857. Again there were no children and after the death of Mrs Agnes Drake in May 1889, Mr Wickham-Drake's cousin, Alfred Henry Tarleton inherited. The house was let for a few years to W.S. Gilbert of Gilbert and Sullivan fame. A character called Shadbolt in *The Yeomen of the Guard* is thought to be named after the owner of Harefield cement works. The Gilberts were fond of children and gave the annual school treat in the grounds. A grand display of fireworks brought a highly enjoyable day to a close in 1889.

THE HOUSE
Although a house has probably stood on the site of Breakspears from medieval times, the present building is mainly seventeenth and eighteenth century in date, with large late-Victorian extensions; but some reused late-16th century work is visible in the hall fireplace and in the glass quarries in the windows.

69. *The chauffeur outside Breakspears about 1921. The doorway still retained its early eighteenth century hood. The relatively new door is embellished with the Tarleton crest.*

The dining-room fireplace has a carving of an ash tree with a B and a Y on either side, the Ashby rebus. This pun on the family name is repeated on a monument in the chancel of St Mary's. Captain Tarleton's smoking room and enlarged drawing room at one end and new domestic offices at the other, give the house an extremely plain and unbalanced appearance on the north-east side, especially since the main door lost its shell hood (*c.*1700) sometime after 1923. The main door had been on the south-east front, reached by a drive from Harvil Road.

A warm red brick dovecote, built in an orchard in the early seventeenth century stands in the grounds not far from the house, but in a sad state of decay. There is a clock on the cupola.

COMMANDER TARLETON

Alfred H. Tarleton, son of Admiral Sir Walter Tarleton, joined the Royal Navy in 1874 at the age of 12. He left the Active List in 1888 when he married Henrietta Tennyson d'Eyncourt, daughter of another admiral, and a year or two later came to reside in Harefield.

In 1913 still on the Emergency List, he was promoted to the position of Commander and was equerry to the Duke of Albany. He improved the house, beautified the estate and played a prominent part in village affairs. The attractive lodge, stable block and staff cottage along Breakspear Road were erected in typical 'improving landlord' style about 1904 and the former poorhouse cottages in Breakspear Road, south of the Spotted Dog, were doubled in size by the addition of wings, one dated 1892 and the other embellished with the Tarleton crest in 1909. The estate had reached its zenith and with the Newdigates absent from Harefield and owning little land in the parish at that date, Captain Tarleton was able to adopt the role of country squire. Some old Harefield residents reminiscing in the 1970s remembered him as a somewhat arrogant and autocratic figure, demanding such marks of respect as tugging of forelocks by boys and curtseys from girls.

However he was viewed by the villagers, he certainly had their interests at heart. In 1896 he presented the males of the village with the Breakspear Institute, run as a Working Men's Club, where they could improve their minds in the reading room and rest their bodies in the smoking room. There was even a bathroom "with full lavatorial equipment", which must have been a luxury for most members. Tea and mineral water was supplied. The Institute was intended to lure the men out of those rival attractions the fourteen village pubs.

From 1891 Tarleton sat on the local bench at Uxbridge, helping to preserve law and order in the neighbourhood, though his public-spiritedness was almost certainly not appreciated by those locals who eked out their rations by poaching. He served the Parish Council as vice-chairman from its inception at the end of 1894 until 1904. As an extension of his public service he took an interest in the Boy Scout movement and became County Commissioner for Middlesex in 1913, nobly allowing the first Middlesex County Camp for between 500 and 600 boys to be held at Breakspears at Whitsun the following year.

The Tarletons lived in great state at Breakspears with twelve indoor and seventeen outdoor servants and entertained lavishly. Members of the royal family planted commemorative trees in the grounds. In 1913 the Tarletons celebrated their silver wedding with balls on successive days, one for the principal residents of the neighbourhood and one for the house-

70. *Commander Alfred H. Tarleton. He was a practical man who kept a private fire engine at Breakspears, in the care of the estate carpenter, which was lent out on occasion to douse neighbouring fires.*

71. *The new lodge in Breakspear Road, built in 1904 about the same time as a new drive was laid out. Previously, the way into the house had been up the long drive from Harvil Road.*

72. The old Spotted Dog on Breakspear Road about 1920. The old poorhouse, later converted into two cottages bearing the Tarleton crest, stands to the south.

73. *Warren Farm, Breakspear Road, a site used by Middlesex scouts in 1915.*

74. *Shepherds Hill House in Northwood Road has a Regency style verandah. The house was purchased by Joseph Ashby Partridge and his sister, Anne, lived there with four servants until her death in 1855. It was known as the Dower House in Commander Tarleton's day. After the Second World War the London County Council bought it and used it as a Nurses' Home. Subsequently it was neglected for many years until the Inner London Education Authority converted it into a Residential Study Centre for primary school children in 1986. The centre continues to function under a different funding body.*

hold and tenants. When Captain Tarleton died in June 1921 workers from the estate carried his coffin over the fields from Breakspears to the church.

In 1936 terms of a sales agreement were drawn up with the Middlesex County Council, for Breakspears House and Langley, Knightscote and Bourne Farms. £30,525 were paid for the 572 acres.[3] Mrs Tarleton was to be tenant for life; after her death in 1951, the house was taken over by Harrow local authority and an old people's home was established there in 1956. It was closed in 1987 and has stood empty ever since.

Harefield Park

Harefield Park, now world famous as Harefield Hospital, was the creation of Sir George Cooke (1675-1740), prothonotary of the Court of Common Pleas. He came to Harefield after his marriage to Anne Jennings, daughter of Edward Jennings, later Counsel to Queen Anne, in 1700. He purchased Rythes, once the home of John Pritchett, Bishop of Gloucester, from John Stanyon, the bishop's son-in-law, in 1705 and an old house called variously Bellhammonds, Belhackets or Godfreys situated near the top of Mill Lane (now Park Lane) shortly afterwards. He built a new mansion in 1710 called Rythes. Overs and Beechfield, a small group of cottages standing about where Mount Pleasant is today, were included in the sale. They seem to have been demolished and the land thrown into the park. Mill Lane, the road to the mill, ran a little north of the present Park Lane and went around the cottages. At that point another road led from Mill Lane to Eversden (now Black

75. (Below) Harefield Park before the First World War. Although there have been alterations to the windows, this is the house rebuilt by George Cooke about 1740. In the 1990s, stripped of its creeper and painted cream, it is the Doctors' Residence at Harefield Hospital.

76. (Top right) Map showing the position of the road to the mill in the early eighteenth century before Overs and Beechfield were demolished and the line of the lane (now Park Lane) moved further south. (Based on GLRO Acc. 1085 EM 14)

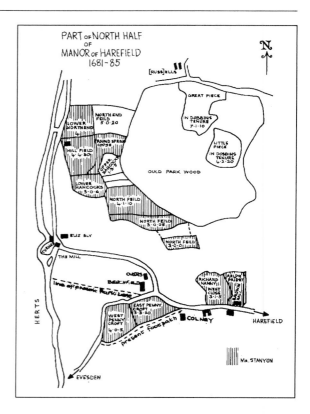

77. The stable block at Harefield Park adorned by the Cooke family crest.

78. Colneys Farm. The farmhouse was rebuilt east of its original site, sometime after being purchased by George Cooke in 1752.

Jack's Cottage) by the river. The line can be seen today as a hollow way wending across Coppermill Down.

Cooke's son, another George (1709-68), also prothonotary of the Court of Common Pleas, was related by marriage to Sir Roger Newdigate and purchased a large chunk of the demesne from him in 1752, including the mills (see chapter 9), part of Colneys Farm, Shepherds Hill Farm, Dobbins House (later Harefield House) and Bayhurst and Old Park Wood.[1] He extended his park as far as the footpath that still leads down to Eversden and bought Eversden itself and a fishery belonging to it from the Ashbys in 1758. His legal business appears to have brought in plenty of money because he practically rebuilt his father's great house, renaming it Bellhammonds for a time before reverting to Rythes. His prosperity is evident from his will[2] written in 1764 (he died in 1768), which mentions the manor of Hayes and land in Southall, his chambers in Hare Court, Inner Temple, and a house in Lincoln's Inn Fields, as well as the Harefield property. The town house was embellished with many original paintings, antique porphyry busts, bronzes and a marble figure of Morpheus

on a pedestal of rock work. The china was decorated with his coat-of-arms. He provided for his children and exhorted them to attend his body to the grave, "and not according to the shameful custom that prevails leave my body to be exposed to the care of servants only and the mercy of an undertaker". Despite these remarks he trusted his servants and left them many bequests. Elizabeth Soanes "who has diligently and carefully nursed me during my frequent and severe fits of illness" received £100 and a year's wages, some silver ware, an eight-day clock and a dwelling called Biddles in Harefield Street.

His son and grandson were both soldiers. General Sir George Cooke, his grandson, who lost an arm at Waterloo, changed the name of the house to Harefield Park. He died unmarried in 1837 and was succeeded by his brother, Sir Henry Frederick Cooke, who enjoyed the estate for only five weeks before dying himself. There being no direct heirs, his nephew William Frederick Vernon inherited and for about twenty years the house was let to tenants. One was Dr Thomas Wakley, editor of *The Lancet* and medical reformer. When Mr Vernon finally moved to Harefield himself in the 1860s, he threw himself into local affairs and privately published his *Notes on the Parish of Harefield*. The beer-house at Hill End was named the Vernon Arms in his honour. His rather reclusive brother, Lt-Gen. George Augustus Vernon succeeded him in 1889 and *his* son, Bertie Wentworth Vernon of Stoke Bruerne, who seems to have been in financial trouble, became involved in a series of property transactions, first mortgaging a large part of the estate, then buying new property, which was mortgaged in its turn and finally selling off land piecemeal. He sold the house and park and much else to John Gutzmer Hossack in 1908.[3]

The house had been leased to Charles Billyard-Leake of New South Wales from 1898. He and his wife Letitia were very sociable and having laid out

a cricket pitch near the rose garden, frequently raised a team to play local matches. Their skating parties on the lake each winter have passed into folk memory. They purchased the house and park from Mr Hossack in 1909 and upon the outbreak of war in 1914, offered it to the Minister of Defence of New South Wales "to be used as a home for convalescent soldiers of the AIF (Australian Imperial Force) for the period of the war and six months afterwards".

HAREFIELD HOSPITAL[4]

Miss Ethel Gray and four other nursing sisters organised the conversion of the country house to a hospital. Huts were erected on the lawns and eighty beds were ready when the first patients arrived on 2 June 1915. Huts sprouted all over the grounds as more than 1000 beds were eventually needed. The wounded soldiers became a familiar site in the village and became friendly with the children. They dropped in unexpectedly on cottagers and were usually welcomed, but occasionally lone ladies were a little frightened by the informality.

The military hospital closed in January 1920, but already the Middlesex County Council had taken steps to purchase it and convert it into a tuberculosis

79. *Thomas Wakley, medical reformer and editor of The Lancet magazine. (From the Illustrated London News, June 1862).*

80. *Huts built on the lawns of Harefield Park to accommondate wounded soldiers of the Australian Imperial Force, during the First World War.*

81. *Patients at the Military Hospital with a pet wallaby.*

82. *A Church Parade in 1917. Soldiers who were fit enough attended morning service at St Mary's. The whole village seems to have come out to watch the spectacle. The Breakspear Institute, almost opposite the hospital gates, is on the right.*

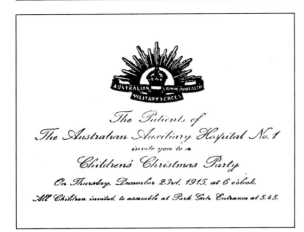

83. *The Australians mixed with the villagers and played a part in local society. The children's Christmas party was one of many activities.*

hospital. It opened as the Harefield County Sanatorium in October 1921. Such was the fear of tuberculosis at the time that the villagers were far from welcoming and children were warned to stay well away from the site. The temporary pavilions where patients lived more or less in the open air, were created out of the old huts and regarded as temporary. The main block of the permanent hospital opened in 1937.

Part of St Mary's Hospital moved out from Paddington on the outbreak of the Second World War, and although the sanatorium continued, thoracic and general surgical services were developed. Tuberculosis declined in the years following the war and Harefield continued with thoracic surgery and developed the cardiac surgery for which it is now famous.

The house built by George Cooke about 1740 still stands and is used as a doctors' residence.

84. *Harefield County Sanatorium. The new permanent buildings were opened by the Duke of Gloucester on 8 October 1937. This was the last hospital to be built in Britain before the Second World War. The stable of the old house can be seen on the extreme left and Old Park Wood at top left.*

85. Guttersdean (now Harefield Grove) substantially as rebuilt between 1836-60 by Stephen Morgan, a Russia Merchant.

Lesser Estates

HAREFIELD GROVE (formerly GUTTERSDEAN)

Guttersdean was mentioned in manor court rolls as early as 1518, when it belonged to the Bynchesters. It stood on the edge of the common set back from the Rickmansworth Road, then a track across the waste. The enclosed fields belonging to it spread behind towards Tosses Lane (now Northwood Road), amounting to sixty acres in the 1630s when Joanne Ashby was in possession.[1] After the death of Joanne's daugher Alice Lynde, it passed through the hands of several owners, mostly absentees, and the house was occupied by yeomen. At the end of the seventeenth century Daniel Coggs of Denham let it to James Starkey who was living there with his third wife, Sarah and five children in 1699 when Gregory King surveyed Harefield. James aged 22 was the first wife's son, 15-year-old John's mother had been the second wife and Sarah's three children were 7, 5 and

2. A male and female servant completed the household. Shortly afterwards James Starkey seems to have fallen on hard times and when Sarah died of smallpox in 1707, the younger children were fostered by the Bugberds of Hill End, at the expense of the parish.[2]

Edward Jennings of the Inner Temple, who was related by marriage to the Cookes of Harefield Park replaced the old farmhouse with a gentleman's residence in plain style about 1752. One of his servants was "John Beasley, a black" who was baptised at St Mary's at the age of 18. Jennings died in 1774 and for the next 200 years the small country estate attracted a series of mainly resident owners who played a part in local affairs, attending the parish vestry and sitting on the local bench. The next owner of note was the Revd Edward Barnard who came to Harefield in 1801 and was minister at the church from 1803-1808. He changed the name from the intriguing Guttersdean to the more prosaic Harefield Grove.

Stephen Morgan, a Russia merchant spent the years from 1836 to 1860 at the Grove and substantially rebuilt it. He was followed by Robert Barnes, a

86. The staff at Harefield Grove early this century.

former Lord Mayor of Manchester who only stayed for a few years, but made his mark on Harefield by building a Methodist chapel in the village and a Memorial Hall. According to an advertisement for the sale by auction in 1868 when Mr Barnes was leaving, the house was "situate in the midst of charming and diversified scenery, excellent society and proverbially healthy locality....suitable for a family of distinction." It was purchased by a distiller, Joseph Boord.

In the 1880s Harefield Grove was considered "the foremost place in England for horticulture" according to the local paper, when George Webster was running a market garden there. Bananas, nectarines, peaches, grapes, tomatoes and cucumbers were displayed at Harefield horticultural show. Mr Webster bankrupted himself in 1896 when his mineral water factory at Springwell failed and Bertie Wentworth Vernon acquired his house. Mr and Mrs Bertram Pemberton Stedall leased Harefield Grove from him in 1907 and later bought it. She was an ardent suffragette and addressed public meetings on the village green, to the disgust of Charlie Filkins and Charles 'Snapper' Brown who planned to throw her into the pond.

The last private family at the Grove was that of Rowland Wilton Cox, whose company manufactured car parts and tubular steel furniture. They moved there in 1936. Mrs Cox moved on to Woodcock Hill House (formerly known as Harefield Grove Farm)

after her husband's death in 1961 and the big house remained empty and became increasingly dilapidated. Several films were made on location there, *Black Beauty* and *The Professionals* among them.[3] Initial Plc took over the house and grounds in 1982. They restored and extended it, making it into prestigious offices. The company has since moved out.

HAREFIELD HOUSE
Harefield House, standing slightly back from the High Street, has also become a company headquarters. Country & Metropolitan Estates thoroughly renovated the house in 1994 in return for planning permission for a housing estate in the gardens. The survey and work uncovered buildings of five different periods going back to a timber-framed cottage of 16th century date.

It stands on the edge of the former heathland that extended down the east side of the street and the earliest reference is to a tenement held from the lord of the manor by Thomas Bickington in 1593. A close called Ferranders went with it and by 1602 that was the name of the house. Richard Bateman, bailiff to Lord Chandos lived there in 1674 and on his death two years later, his son-in-law, Richard Dobbins purchased "Ferranders or Beckingtons" for £250 from the newly-returned Sir Richard Newdigate. Dobbins fell out with the next Sir Richard by objecting to the deposition of Roger Davies, the minister, and joining

87. *Harefield House incorporates work of five periods, going back to a cottage of the sixteenth century, owned by Thomas Bickington. It was largely rebuilt by the Newdigates c.1750. The gardens were laid out in the 1920s by H. Avray-Tipping, architect and landscape gardener.*

in the struggle on Davies' behalf on the Sunday when the battle of the feather dusters was waged (see Chapter 1). He was financially ruined by litigation over the position of churchwarden which he believed should have been his, but for Sir Richard exerting undue influence over his tenants. Fortunately, his earlier career as a soldier enabled him to apply to become a Poor Knight of Windsor. (The knights were created in 1352 to pray in St George's Chapel for the souls of the sovereign and the Knights of the Garter.) According to the citation he had personally served Charles II at the battle of Worcester and been obliged to flee overseas "to the utter ruin of his family".[4] Sir Richard repurchased Dobbins House and his tenant Thomas Topping was there in 1699. Later he leased it to his son-in-law, Abraham Meure of Westminster.

COUNT BRUHL[5]

Count Bruhl was appointed Saxon envoy to the Court of St James in 1764 and bought Dobbins House which had been rebuilt about 1750 and renamed Harefield House a little later, from Sir Roger Newdigate. He married the widowed Countess Egremont in 1767 and they raised a family in Harefield. The count's major interests were in science and astronomy and he built an observatory at the house. He experimented in chronometry as well, which probably en-

88. *Count Bruhl, Saxon Envoy to the Court of St James, whose interest in astronomy led him to erect an observatory at Harefield House; George III visited him there to examine "Bruhl's gadgets"*

89. A school function taking place in the grounds of Harefield House c.1920. Church fêtes were also held there.

couraged George III, another amateur chronometrist, to take dinner with him at his country residence in the summer of 1788 to take a look at "Bruhl's gadgets". The visit was recorded by Fanny Burney in her diary. The king's uncertain mental state showed that night when he made peculiar remarks about the music stands used by the small orchestra that was playing in the observatory and took exception to black and white Wedgewood vases with holes in them, which he said "looked like skulls".

THE BYLES FAMILY & H. AVRAY-TIPPING

Philip Champion de Crespigny lived at Harefield House from 1809 to 1851 and after a few years the Byles moved in. Sir John Byles (1801-84) was a judge of the Court of Common Pleas and became famous for a legal tome known as "Byles on Bills". His son Walter, a barrister, was a member of the first Middlesex County Council in 1888 and Lord Lieutenant in 1896. He was a trustee of the Memorial Hall and manager of the parish school and churchwarden. When he died in 1921, the same year as Captain Tarleton, the house was sold to H. Avray-Tipping, a well-known architect and landscape gardener.

Mr Tipping was on the editorial staff of *Country*

90. *Walter Barnard Byles of Harefield House sat on the Uxbridge Bench, was a member of the first Middlesex County Council and Lord Lieutenant of the county.*

91. *'Apple Trees' and 'Pear Trees', the two smaller houses designed by H. Avray-Tipping and standing in the grounds of Harefield House on the Breakspear Road frontage.*

Life. He made the gardens of Harefield House the envy of the neighbourhood, employing ten gardeners. They were thrown open from time to time in aid of local charities and church fêtes and sales of work were held there. He was an authority on ordinary as well as great houses and designed four 'average' houses built in his grounds in 1933. Two of them were planned as 'servantless houses' and two were considerably larger with four bedrooms and two bathrooms. Three still stand in Breakspear Road behind the old perimeter wall of the estate. The other was demolished to make way for Pond Close. Unmarried, he left the house to his long-time retainer Walter Wood when he died in 1933. Mr Wood gave

92. 'Walnut Trees', one of the larger houses, which was demolished to make way for Pond Close. Little Hammonds, the other larger house, still stands.

93. Ickenham Hall in Glebe Avenue was the former Sherwyns, home of John Crosier who died in 1769. A house has stood on this site since at least 1416. The Crosiers were in possession by 1624.

94. *Home Farm, Ickenham. The gabled house on the left has a fifteenth-century timber frame with finely moulded spandrels and moulded beams. The brick-built wing on the right has the initials W C (possibly William Crosier) and the date 1705 incised in the brickwork. It is almost certainly the house called Church Place in a survey of 1624. The name, Home Farm, only came into use in 1887. Matthew Saich, licensee of the Coach & Horses, leased Home Farm from the Hilliards in the 1870s. His grandson, Cyril Saich, purchased it in 1927 and lived there until his death in 1989. During 1993-4 warden-controlled units were built on the field adjoining the farmhouse. The old name Church Place has been revived for the new estate.*

some land for the Cricket Club and built a new house on the Breakspear Road frontage, but soon put the mansion up for sale and left Harefield in 1936. It was advertised as a "charming, old-fashioned gentleman's residence", but was bought by the government to be used by the Air Ministry as a Test House of the Aeronautical Inspection Directorate.

AERONAUTICAL QUALITY INSURANCE DIRECTORATE

Staff from the two existing test houses at Cardington and Kidbrooke moved to Harefield in October 1938. A new laboratory building was erected in the grounds and the title was changed from Aeronautical Inspection Directorate to Aeronautical Quality Insurance Directorate and the house was subsequently known as AQD. The house and site were vacated in February 1988. The new housing development on the site of the laboratory and outbuildings, is called Wellington Place because Wellington bombers were tested here during the war.

SHERWYNS/SHEERINGS

So much of Ickenham was swallowed up by the manorial estates, especially Swakeleys, that there was only one other estate of importance. It was based on the present Ickenham Hall and owned by the Crosiers.

The Compass Theatre in Glebe Avenue, Ickenham, is built onto a house of mid-eighteenth century appearance. The brick wall outside is older and some timbers inside suggest that an earlier building was remodelled in Georgian times. It was called Sherwyns in 1769 when John Crosier referred to it in his will[6] and the name derives from John Cherwynd's

95. *The Home and Tipper Farms' float being driven through Uxbridge on an Uxbridge Agricultural Show day. Cyril Saich is driving.*

96. Ickenham Hall was turned into a Youth Centre by the Middlesex County Council in 1948 and the Compass Theatre was built onto it in the 1960s.

messuage mentioned in a court roll of 1416. The new name of Ickenham Hall was adopted when the Shorediches' manor house dropped it and became Manor Farm.

CROSIERS AND HILLIARDS

The Crosiers were major landowners in north-west Middlesex and were established in Ickenham in the sixteenth century. They owned Church Place (almost certainly Home Farm), Sherwyns and Sears in 1624. Michael Crosier bought Reynolds Close near Sherwyns in 1628 and a house and barn were built on it, which became the home farm attached to the house. William Crosier purchased Rayners (later Milton Farm) from John Carwitham in 1685. After the enclosure of 1780 John Crosier caused Hill Farm to be erected on his newly enclosed land in the former Brook Mead. All this property descended to Edward

Hilliard Junior in 1801. He was the second son of John Crosier's niece, Elizabeth Stafford Crosier who had married George Hilliard, a lawyer in 1779.[7]

The Hilliards sold off their land piecemeal. Milton Farm became part of the Swakeleys estate in 1816. and Hill Farm was incorporated in Northolt Aerodrome in 1916. Cyril Saich who died in 1989, whose family moved into Home Farm in the 1890s, purchased it from the Hilliards in 1927. Ickenham Hall was sold to the Metropolitan Railway Company in 1902 and was bought by Charles de Winton Kitcat after the line was opened in 1904. Nearby Lawrence Drive honours Dame Maude Lawrence, Director of Women's Establishments at the Treasury who lived at Ickenham Hall until her death in 1933. Middlesex County Council took it over and turned it into a Youth Centre in 1948 and it became the Compass Community Arts Centre in the 1960s.

Caring for the Poor

PRIVATE CHARITY

Providing for the poor was a christian duty and most medieval people who were sufficiently well endowed left money or goods for them. John Girdler who was probably a citizen of London with Harefield connections, and died in 1402, wanted sixty poor men and women to have a penny each on the day of his interment at St Peter's, Westminster (Westminster Abbey) and one hundred poor men and women in Harefield to have the same. This figure was about a quarter of the poulation at the time. John Ashby, son of George Ashby who was Clerk of the Signet to Queen Margaret, was buried at Rickmansworth in 1499. He willed "That my body be closed in canvas price the ell 4d and above that be covered with linen cloth, price the ell 8d and at the time of the laying of my body into the earth I will that the lynnon cloth of 8d be taken off and dyvyded into 4 parts and given unto 4 pore men or women after the discrecon of my executors". More acceptable perhaps were the twelve shirts and smocks of good strong canvas, ordered by William Say of Ickenham in 1582 to "be prepared against Good Friday next after my decease", to be given to six men and six women of the poorest households.

THE PARISH

The 1601 Poor Law placed the burden of looking after the poor on the parish, which was obliged to provide a place of asylum for the aged and infirm, give work to the able-bodied poor and apprentice poor children to a trade. The scheme was financed by a rate levied on property and administered by officials known as overseers of the poor, working within the framework of the vestry. Occasional payments were made in times of necessity, and food, clothing, fuel and nursing care provided. Cottage rents were sometimes paid, but eventually very poor families were moved into a poor house. The chronically sick and those past their labour became parish pensioners.

HOUSING THE POOR

An old messuage known as Ruffins standing on the west side of Harefield High Street had been divided into four by 1630 and one part seems to have been used as a poor house later in the century. It stood between the Cricketers and the Rose and Crown. Gregory King described six families living there in 1699, 21 people in all, with the mentally unstable Grace Read and her son William among them. She had been abandoned by her husband and had already spent about six months in Bedlam at parish expense and had to be restrained by being chained to a post for a time after her return. She received

97. The King's Arms, Harefield has been an inn since the seventeenth century, although the building is older. William Iley, the landlord from the 1680s until his death in 1708, often supplied goods for the poor.

98. Ruffins lay between the Rose & Crown on the left of the picture and the Cricketers which is tucked back out of sight — the sign in the road indicates its position. The furthest part of Ruffins was rebuilt and had become Somerville's, the bakers, by 1871 (the tallest building). The middle section was rebuilt a little later. The portion nearest to the Rose & Crown appears to be still standing when this photograph was taken in about 1919. The four cottages "builded on the waste" in the seventeenth century stood opposite.

a regular pension from the parish and died of small-pox in 1707.[1]

Other inmates were Abell and Sarah Spakeman with their five younger children. Abell's grandfather had been deputy-steward of the manor in the Countess of Derby's time and his father had been Keeper for Sir Richard Newdigate, but although he himself was educated and did odd jobs, like helping Gregory King with his surveying, he could not keep his family without parish help. In 1700 he became parish clerk on a small salary, but his son Nathan died in 1708, then his wife in 1710 and he himself in 1712. His children (more had been born since 1699) were fostered and apprenticed. Rebecca was sent to Colham Green, but ran away, whether because she was cruelly treated or simply homesick for Harefield is not known, but the overseers sent her back to her master. Several other payments were made relating to apprenticeships for "Spakeman's Garl", probably another of his daughters. The girls were most likely being apprenticed as domestic servants. The accounts make no mention of a trade.[2]

COTTAGES FOR THE POOR

The heath came down the east side of Harefield Street as far as Dobbins House in the seventeenth century and four cottages "were erected and builded on the waste" for "the relief of certain poor people of the

parish". They were let by the lord of the manor at such very low rents as 8 shillings a year, whereas 20 or 30 shillings was the more usual sum. Presumably the buildings were very small and were thatched with straw. John Bazley was paid 14 shillings for "thotchin the poores housen" and Robert Trenley 13 shillings "for stra for ye poores houses" about 1713.[3] Cottages for the poor were built on the edge of the heath in Breakspear Road in 1800. They cost just over £99 to build. £77 came from the poor rate and the rest from interest on stock invested in compensation for land taken from the moor by the Canal Company a few years earlier. They still stand, having been later added to and converted into workers cottages for the Breakspear estate.

WORKHOUSE[4]

A workhouse, still standing as a private house, was built close by in 1782. John Rowe, one of the overseers of the poor, used his own horse and cart to move paupers into the house in March 1783. Some may have come from the older cottages, but others had been lodged at the expense of the parish, at the King's Arms, where John Burbidge was the innkeeper. The governor of the workhouse contracted to feed and clothe the poor for an annual sum, paid monthly. He made what profit he could from the garden produce and paupers' work. Charles Cox of Harrow-on-the

99. *Harefield Workhouse, now a private house in Breakspear Road, was erected on the edge of the heath in 1782. It housed between twenty and thirty paupers in the early years. From 1836, the poor went to the Uxbridge Union Workhouse at Hillingdon.*

Hill agreed to farm the poor of Harefield for £1068 in 1821 and by 1830 the governor was allowed 4s 3d per week for each inmate. There were thirteen people in the house in December 1831, but numbers fluctuated according to agricultural conditions and the amount of out-relief being paid by the overseers. Between 20 and 30 had been the usual number in earlier years.

Following the passing of the Poor Law Amendment Act of 1834 Harefield became part of Uxbridge Union. Paupers from Harefield, Ickenham and Northolt were lodged at Ruislip in August 1836, so that the small parish workhouses could be sold to raise money for a new Union House, which was opened at Hillingdon two years later. Harefield workhouse was sold to Joseph Ashby Partridge of Breakspears who converted it into five cottages. James Milton, who was born in the 1840s, spent most of his life in one of them. After working as a gardener first at Breakspears, then for the Hulls of Uxbridge and for the Revd Beauchamp Pell at Ickenham, he returned to the old workhouse and established a market garden on the adjoining land. He grew geraniums,

arum lilies, lilacs and tomatoes, then only just becoming popular, and sold much of his produce at Covent Garden. He became a parish councillor in 1894 and was a trustee of the Methodist church. After the death of Captain Tarleton in 1921 Douglas Brown a local cattle dealer bought the cottages. By 1953 they were condemned and due for demolition, but were rescued by Dorothy and Walter Winton who gradually turned them back into a charming single house and lived there for nearly 40 years.

ICKENHAM

The Revd John Addison answering the queries of the Poor Law Commissioners in 1832 remarked upon the small extent of the parish, which meant that the real necessities of applicants for poor relief were well known to the overseers. There was a poor house with a garden on the roadside waste just outside the churchyard, which had been there since before1780, but the exact date of erection is unknown. The parish cage stood beside it. After 1836 it was pulled down and the site was thrown into the churchyard. The

100. Buntings, Ickenham, the home of John Henry Gell and his wife Charlotte. The place is first mentioned in the fifteenth century, but this house appears to date from the late eighteenth century. The Cochran family (daughter and son-in-law of Thomas Truesdale Clarke) lived there in Victorian times. The present Buntings, part of a Sheltered Housing Scheme, was built in 1920 and the cellars of the old house form a sunken garden at the side.

101. Little Buntings was built after 1835 on the garden ground of Ickenham Poorhouse. Mr Fassnidge of Uxbridge built it for John Henry Gell. It was used as an annex to Buntings in the Cochrans' time. The site of the poorhouse itself was thrown into the churchyard.

garden ground was sold for £30 to John Henry Gell of Buntings, who had Little Buntings built there by Mr Fassnidge, the Uxbridge builder.

ALMSHOUSES[5]

Both Harefield and Ickenham have delightful almshouses still in use.

The group in Church Hill, Harefield were built soon after 1637 under the terms of the Countess of Derby's will. The 'hospital' was to house six poor women, presided over by a master who would read prayers for them, and each inmate was to receive a pension of £5 a year. The women had their own rooms and the master, who was intended to be the minister of the church, had two rooms. He seems to have been expected to run a school there as well, although this was not stipulated in Lady Alice's will. As already seen in Chapter 4, later ministers were not resident. There was a communal wash-house and bake-house. Feelings ran high if places were allo-

cated to strangers born outside Harefield and the villagers sometimes petitioned the lord of the manor on behalf of a candidate. "...That the widow Kneaton may goo into that almeshouse the which Elizabeth Robbeson late dyed in for we all think her the fittest person being very aiged and hath been a widow a long time". In 1699 two of the almswomen had children living with them and one a grandchild.

The almshouses nearly suffered the dreadful fate of demolition in 1954, when there were only two residents, but they were restored in 1959 and four ladies now occupy the ground floor.

In Ickenham, Charlotte Gell of Buntings gave land from her grounds to build a row of five almshouses in Back Lane in 1857, shortly after her husband's death. She intended them firstly for retired servants who had lived in the Gell family for at least five years and then for Ickenham inhabitants, who must be members of the Church of England. No more than three people were to live in one dwelling. The

102. *The Dowager Countess of Derby's Almshouses in Church Hill, Harefield, were built under the terms of her will, dated 1637. Her coat-of-arms on a widow's lozenge (only men bore a shield) can be seen above the central door. The upper floor has been empty since the restoration of the 1950s, not being considered safe for habitation.*

ICKENHAM CHURCH & PUMP

103. Charlotte Gell's pump. It is hard to imagine the centre of Ickenham without the pump under its decorative canopy. The well was sunk in 1866 under the terms of Mrs Gell's will. She died in 1863.

104. Ickenham Cottages were built by Charlotte Gell of Buntings in 1857 for retired servants of the Gell family and the inhabitants of Ickenham. These attractive residences in the centre of Ickenham are lived in and administered by the church.

inmates of each house were to have £20 a year to share between them. The almshouses have been restored in recent years and are administered by the church.

Mrs Gell directed in her will that a well should be sunk in the centre of the village and a pump erected over it. This pump under its decorative canopy is a feature of modern Ickenham and a regular meeting place. She also left money for coal to be distributed at Christmas.

THE POOR'S LAND

Solomon Burbury, a patten sole and last maker of London, gave the rent of Littlewoods in Breakspear Road to the poor of Harefield by his will of 1697. The house on the site is now the Dairy Farm.

More poor's land, twenty acres on Tosses Lane (now Northwood Road), was set aside by the enclosure commissioners in 1813, in lieu of the rights of poor cottagers to cut furze and bushes on the common for fuel. It was rented and the rent paid for fuel for such of the poor as did not receive parish relief. Other sums were left in wills to be invested and the income expended on the poor. Mrs Mary Ashby left £100 in 1664; Mrs Charlotte Williams, daughter of William Ashby left £600 in 1793, for bread to be given out on Sundays between May and September and all the year round to the almswomen; John Ashford who had been a confidential servant to Sir Christopher Baynes of Harefield Place, in 1857 left £600 for meat, bread, fuel and clothes for the aged poor; Henry Goodman left £500 in 1858 for flour, raisins and beer for fifty families. The charities were amalgamated by the Charity Commissioners in 1879 and mostly administered as coal charities thereafter, but beer continued to be dispensed under the terms of the Goodman charity. Some ministers complained about the drunkeness that ensued on Christmas Eve and in 1930 the beer money was appropriated for cleaning the schoolroom!

105. *The pond which is such a feature of modern Ickenham was enlarged to take the waste water from the pump. Church Farm can be seen behind the telegraph pole.*

106. *The Dairy Farm stands on the poor's land, once called Littlewoods.*

107. Cripps Farm down Springwell Lane stands near a former piece of common called Birchin Green. The sixteenth-century timber-framed house was given a brick skin and extended, probably in the late eighteenth century.

Farming the Land

COMMON FIELDS

Common fields, large areas divided into strips and farmed by numbers of villagers, existed in both Ickenham and Harefield, but those in Harefield had mostly disappeared by the sixteenth century. In Ickenham there were five such fields which lay to the south of the village – Home, Middle, Further, Blackhill and Tottingworth Fields. In 1649 eight Ickenham residents farmed parts of these fields in which wheat, peas and beans were the main crops. In Harefield in 1546 the owners of Rythes and Westons – down the bottom of Mill (now Park) Lane – both held land in North Field and Hill Field. The occupants of Weybeards, north of the heath, Aylmots near Cripps Farm and Arnolds down Mill Lane, had a few acres each in North Field. These five farms were all on the north-west side of Harefield. North Dean Farm on the bank of the Colne, along Summerhouse Lane, may have been created out of the former Hill Field and is mentioned first in 1564. John Stanyon of Rythes bought it in the seventeenth century and it was later part of the Cookes' Harefield Park estate and was possibly renamed Summerhouse.

THE COMMONS

The heath and moors were owned by the lords of the manors though many village people had specific common rights over them. In Harefield, the extensive heath was used for rough grazing and fuel cutting but was gradually encroached upon near Harefield Street and in the eighteenth and nineteenth centuries men are noted in the court rolls for erecting hoghouses, carthouses and cottages without licence there. Usually they were ordered to pull them down, but at a subsequent court were permitted "to enjoy" them upon payment of a fine – a form of retrospective planning permission.

The minerals and the fish in the ponds also belonged to the lords of the manors, but occasionally proved too strong a temptation. In 1804 eleven men including three members of the Webb family, were fined 10s 6d each for digging mud from the pond on Harefield common and selling it. One of them was also fined at the same court for fishing the ponds.

108. Weybeards was one of the farms which had land in North Field in the mid-sixteenth century.

HAREFIELD MOOR, COW MOOR, HOG MOOR AND BUNGERS HILL

Over-grazing of the moors was sometimes a problem when people exceeded their permitted use and hogs dug up the ground when they were not properly ringed. Perhaps it was anger at the way pigs damaged the ground that caused Will Batman and Abell Gavell to cut off hogs' noses in 1518 and led to beating and breaking of heads and shedding of blood. Generally, people were supposed to graze no more animals than they were able to maintain on their own land during the winter. Certain farms seem to have annexed bits of moor at an early date. Savay Farm, just over the river in Denham, owned a close of the former Cow Moor in 1546 and about a third of Harefield Moor was enclosed by the lord of the manor about 1590.

Common rights over the moors at the southern end of Harefield – Cow Moor (66 acres), Hog Moor (4½ acres) and Bungers Hill (about 31 acres) – were shared with people from Uxbridge and Denham, though the grazing rights on Cow Moor were restricted to Brackenbury and Copthall Farms and other properties within the Brackenbury estate; Highway Farm and the Dairy House (now Dewes Farm); Denham Court Farm across the river; and the Uxbridge burgage holders. The Dairy House was possibly the *vaccary* (cow pasture) mentioned in the early fifteenth century. The Uxbridge burgage holders alone had rights

in Hog Moor. Bungers Hill was part of the common land that stretched over the boundary into Hillingdon parish and was known as Northolt Common. A dispute in 1565 between the lords of Colham (Uxbridge was in the manor of Colham) and Harefield, ended with the lord of Colham using Bungers Hill for his rabbit warren and the Newdigates keeping the timber (except that needed to repair the warren) and the tenants of Colham and Harefield sharing grazing rights over the whole of Northolt Common.

BEATONSWOOD

In Ickenham, there were three areas of common land, the marsh of eighteen acres beside the Yeading Brook, Ickenham Green (eleven acres) and eleven acres of woodland called Beatonswood at the top end of the Green, used for grazing and the collection of fuel. The Green, now approached by a footpath beside the Soldier's Return, dwindled into little more than a wide track leading to Beatonswood. A cottage later called Beatonswood Farm was already there in the seventeenth century and may have been on the site of a house called Bay Brane at Bedonhill mentioned in Thomas Betts' will in 1463. Some woodland remained in 1780, but does not appear on subsequent maps and two cottages had been built on the edge of the former wood by 1866. The farmhouse also had land across the River Pinn in Harefield and at the

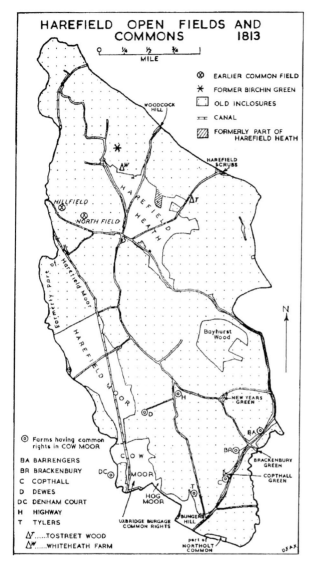

109. Map based on the Enclosure Map of 1813 showing the farms that had grazing rights on Harefield's Cow Moor.

110. A map showing Ickenham's common fields and land use, shortly before enclosure in 1780.

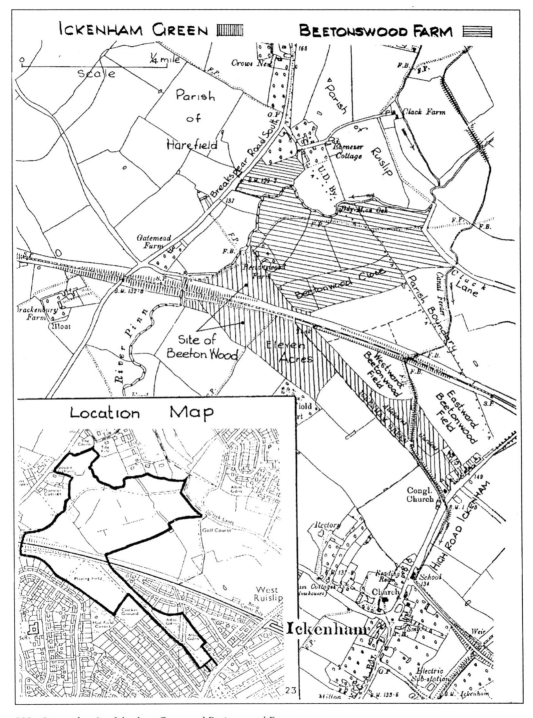

111. A map showing Ickenham Green and Beatonswood Farm.

112. Northwood Road, shown here in 1936, used to be called Tosses Lane, a name derived from a small piece of woodland called Tostreet Wood (see location on illustration 109). The cottage on the left is one of several built on land enclosed from the heath in the years following the Enclosure.

top of Clack Lane in Ruislip amounting to 35 acres at the end of the eighteenth century. In early Victorian times it was the home of the Woodman family and in the 1920s of William Harris, then owner of Glebe Farm. It was sold to the Middlesex County Council in 1936, but demolished in 1946, having been used by Air Raid Wardens during the war. Works to extend Ruislip Golf Course onto Ickenham Green in 1988, encroached upon the old farmyard.

113. Beatonswood Farm – a drawing by Karen Spink based on a photograph taken in the 1920s.

ENCLOSURE OF THE COMMON FIELDS

Over a long period the common fields were gradually enclosed and common rights diminished or else abolished altogether. In Ickenham common fields were enclosed by Act of Parliament in 1780. One new farm, Hill Farm, was created on the former fields, built in 1807 on land allocated to John Crosier and stood where the Control Tower of Northolt Aerodrome is now. A Mr Teak owned it at the beginning of the twentieth century and the airfield extended westwards to take it over in 1916. The Teaks left the house, but continued to farm the land, running sheep over the aerodrome.

At first, most of the newly enclosed land remained arable, but by 1830 much of the land in the parish, both old and new enclosures had been converted to grass. Itinerant haymakers, some from Ireland, became a common phenomenon in Victorian Ickenham. Although hay was a less labour-intensive crop than wheat, peas and beans, a high proportion of Ickenham's inhabitants continued to be employed as agricultural labourers throughout the nineteenth century, there being little alternative without travelling to Uxbridge or Harefield.

The Green and Marsh were left for grazing and in the nineteenth century each householder could turn out one horse or two cows from May Day to Martinmas (11th November). The poorer householders of Ickenham, not possessing large animals, preferred to

114. *Some of the cottages built beside the Soldier's Return at Ickenham Green c.1830*

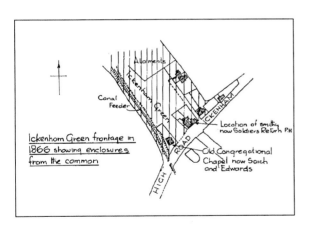

115. *Map showing developments at Ickenham Green after enclosure.*

make allotment gardens on the Green and only the Marsh continued to be used for grazing. The 1834 court rolls record that William Bunce and others on parish relief "...have lately dug up part of the waste for gardens on the Green". At first the gardens were dug without any formal agreement with the lord of the manor. Eventually they agreed to pay one shilling per rood rent, a payment which continued until 1930 when the lease of the Green had passed to Uxbridge Urban District Council and the doughty gardeners refused to pay, claiming squatters' rights.

Several small pieces of waste along the road from Ickenham to Ruislip were enclosed between 1819 and 1835, by permission of George Robinson, then lord of the manor. He himself built a cottage (later the Soldier's Return) and smithy in 1828. The Congregational Chapel (now Saich & Edwards) was built in 1835 on land granted the previous year.

ENCLOSURE IN HAREFIELD

In Harefield the heath and moors were enclosed in 1813 following a Bill promoted by Charles Newdigate-Newdegate, lord of the manor, Sir Christopher Baynes of Harefield Place, Joseph Ashby Partridge of Breakspears and Robert George Spedding of the Coppermills. John Trumper of Harefield, a land surveyor and an experienced Enclosure commissioner was appointed sole commissioner. He caused James Trumper (1787-1859), who was probably his son and also a surveyor, to make a plan of the parish. The Trumpers were prominent in Harefield as farmers as well as surveyors. They leased Dewes, Moorhall, Conduit and Cripps farms in the eighteenth and nineteenth century. Edward, who lived at Conduit Farm (now Manor Court), was village constable in 1784 and had to deal with a dreadful murder at Hill End, when William Walker, who was insane, stabbed his wife Ann with a pocket knife.[1]

In the Act there was no provision for grazing of cattle by former commoners, but the four-acre green was left as a place of recreation for the inhabitants of Harefield and a twenty-acre allotment was set aside for the use of the poor on Northwood Road. The moors produced hay and by 1830 most of the old enclosed farms, using fewer labourers, had converted from arable to hay, which was sold at the London markets, travelling either by road or by canal. Mr Blower, who was born in 1888, remem-

bered accompanying his father on hay carts in the late 1890s. His reminiscences are on tape. "I used to go with him, you see, I was just a boy then....They used to supply the 'bus company and all that, because they was all run by horses, that time of day. Well, it would take about three hours, if you had some good horses. We used to be away at ten o'clock at night

117. This house was known as Marlowes for at least 200 years and became Conduit Farm in the eighteenth century because of a conduit in the field behind. Edward Trumper lived there in the 1780s and Charles Brown, a builder, in Victorian times. Brown extended the house and changed the name to the misleading Manor Court.

116. Harefield Green and pond (known as Shepherd's pond on the Enclosure Map). The green was set aside as a place of recreation for the inhabitants of Harefield. The cottages were built on the former heath.

118. *Haymaking at Ickenham Marsh in Edwardian times. The picture shows the Sims family party helping with the hay as a treat, but haymaking was an important time for poor labouring families, when extra money could be earned to pay for such items as children's boots and shoes.*

as a rule, get down the hay market at about six o'clock when the hay market opened.... We used to stop if a pub opened, because they used to be open all night..."[2] The carts never came back empty, but carried manure from the London stables.

According to the same informant, the former moors and old enclosed land along the Colne were flooded early in March and produced three crops of hay a year instead of one. The flooding made it grow more quickly and the hay was ready five weeks earlier than anywhere else in the parish. 'Floating' the moors may have gone on long before the enclosure. A ditch "to float the Hospital land" is shown on a late eighteenth-century canal map: it ran from the River Colne and fed more ditches surrounding meadows belonging to St Thomas's Hospital where Maple Cross Sewage Works is now (across the river in Hertfordshire). The Hospital owned Savay Farm and had some old enclosed fields called Cowleys in Harefield parish, between the River Colne and Hog Moor Ditch, across the canal from Dewes Farm.

AGRICULTURAL WORKERS

Despite low wages and seasonal unemployment more people worked in agriculture (including market gardening) during most of the nineteenth century than in anything else, as shown in the census returns. There were variations between 38.7% (196 people) of the employed population in Harefield in 1841 and 25.8% (151 people) in 1881, but the percentage was always above the national average. A number of industrial concerns, mainly developed after the building of the Grand Junction Canal, provided alternative work. The number of people with industrial occupations fluctuated with the fortunes of the mills, but exceeded the agricultural workers by 1881. The twenty farms in Harefield in 1813 were still there in 1914, but only twelve were left in 1959. In 1995 Knightscote, Langley, Park Lodge, Highway, Dewes and Whiteheath Farms belong to the Borough of Hillingdon. Park Lodge and Highway Farm were amalgamated in 1962 to create a larger unit known as Park Lodge Farm. The buildings at Highway Farm

119. *Cleaning Harefield pond c.1913. The Swan on the left had been built a few years earlier by Charles Brown, a member of an energetic family that worked Conduit Farm, Park Lodge and Whiteheath Farm in the nineteenth century and ran a building business from Park Place.*

date from the seventeenth and eighteenth centuries and not being suitable for modern farming methods are used for storage and for sheltering sheep in winter and at lambing. The farm manager lives in the lovely red brick house, which has the remains of a moat. Park Lodge farmhouse was converted to a farm interpretation centre in 1974, run at that time by the Greater London Council. Dewes farmhouse is let to tenants, but the land is run as part of Park Lodge. There is a tenant farmer at Knightscote and Langley Farm is occupied by a member of the Council's staff.

Whiteheath Farm still flourishes on the northern edge of the heath. It first appears in a plan of the Breakspear estate, made in 1771. It was the home of the steward until 1800, when it was leased for forty yars to a man called John White. Part of the agreement was that he should build four new rooms on to the front of the building within seven years. Each room was to be not less than 18 feet long, 15 feet wide and 9 feet high. They were to be built with oak and fir timber and brick, with walls two bricks or 18 inches thick up to first floor height and one-and-a-half bricks or 14 inches above. These are the rooms which still appear at the front of Whiteheath farmhouse. Later, the farm passed to the Vernons of Harefield Park and it was let to Charles Brown, the builder. He sub-let to Mr G. Varcoe of London in the 1880s and two weddings followed. Mr Brown's eldest son, Charles, married Miss Frances Varcoe in 1884 and his daughter married Sydney Crook Varcoe in 1893, when the bridesmaids wore cream serge, Paris hats and suede shoes – as reported in the local paper. The farm was conveyed to the Middlesex County Council in 1936..

There were twelve farms in Ickenham in Victorian times. Only Longlane remains as a working farm in 1995 and even worse only two of the other old houses, Manor Farm and Home Farm still stand. Home Farm continued to operate until Cyril Saich died in 1989, but since then the field behind the house has been redeveloped as superior sheltered accommodation, though the house, with particularly good fifteenth century timber work in one wing, has been spared.

120. *John Dalton and his sons stacking straw at Copthall Farm in the 1970s.*

121. *Haymaking at Ickenham Marsh, early this century.*

122. *The cowman at Copthall Farm.*

Earning a Living

FULLING CLOTH

Two mills in Harefield were mentioned in the Domesday Book. They were probably situated on the Colne at the places now called Springwell and Coppermills. The Springwell area was known as Gulchwell in former times, the new name coming into use about 1800. Originally, a well or spring fed the Colney Stream there and was subsequently affected by the canal workings and later quarrying. The plentiful water supply made it a suitable place for a mill. There was certainly one there in 1345 when members of the Ravening family sold 'Ravenyngmyll' to Sir John Swanlond. The siting of this mill at Gulchwell is assumed from the continuity of the name and descriptions in later manorial documents. Richard Aweedon held a tenement called Ravenings "near the fulling mill" in 1510. The house had a garden, some meadow land and moor, a grove by the road from Drakenford (now Draytonford) to Harefield, an eyot and "a watercourse in the river leading from the floodgates of the mill, to the water coming from Gulchwell".[1]

The mention of a fulling mill suggests cloth-making, but as it was close to Rickmansworth, a well-known cloth town, the cloth probably came from there rather than Harefield. Newly woven cloth was scoured to remove oil and size by pounding with gently falling fulling stocks, operated by water power. After drying and the removal of knots and burrs, the cloth was returned to the mill to be laid in soapy water and fulled again to thicken and shrink it. It was dried outside, stretched on tenter frames held in place by tenter hooks. Although references to a fulling mill cease after 1636, the site was probably on the east bank of the Colney Stream in the field named Mill Meadow on the Enclosure Map of 1813. The tenter frames were remembered in the name of the adjoining field, Tenter Meadow.

Deeds connected with the canal in 1797 and 1805, show Union Hall, a house built by James Hunt about 1780, standing on the south side of the road to Draytonford, probably on the site of the old Ravenings, on the opposite side of the stream to the mill site. The name was changed to Springwell Place by 1805 and the house had gone by 1813.

CORN, PAPER AND COPPER

A corn mill belonging to the Harefield lord of the manor existed in the sixteenth century. In 1593 it was leased to John Preest and had a garden and parcel of meadow adjoining in North Field, which suggests that it was on the site of the present

123. Mines Royal House built c.1782 by Mr Cooke of Harefield Park. Robert George Spedding of the Mines Royal Company lived there. The name of the house was changed to Manor House during the occupancy by Mr McCallum of United Asbestos during the 1880s.

Coppermills. There seem to have been two mills owned by the manor in the seventeenth century, a corn mill and a paper mill, the latter being built in 1674. According to a plan made by Gregory King in 1699, both were side by side with a farm along the yard. Edward Carter was then the miller and five men made up the workforce.

When the lord of the manor, Sir Roger Newdigate, sold a large part of his land to George Cooke in 1752, the paper mill, corn mill and Mill Farm were all leased to Richard Ware. Twenty years later there was no mention of the corn mill, but the paper mill and house were in the occupation of Mrs Catherine Ware at £42 per annum. Her lease included the River Colne from "one hundred feet above the Tumbling Bay belonging to the aforesaid mill and runs in two streams on each side of a slip of meadow above the mill and so round the said mill plot where the streams are united and thereon down to the end of the said two meadows lying below the mill as far as the late Mr Ashby's fishery, together with the two weirs erected on the said river for catching fish and the two tumbling bays for keeping the said streams in their proper channels and also the sole right of fishing in all such parts of the said river".[2]

By 1783 George John Cooke had leased the mills and a newly-built mansion house (later known erroneously as the Manor House and restored in 1994) to the Copper Mines Royal for £74 10s rent. The Company leased Troy Mill, also a paper mill at the time, on the Hertfordshire side of the river as well. It is not clear why the Mines Royal Company should need paper mills – perhaps they were investments. Maybe there was already talk of a canal to pass through Harefield which would provide easy transport for copper.

JACK'S MILL

Today there is a restaurant called Black Jack's Mill beside the canal. Contrary to popular opinion this is not an ancient site for a mill. Gregory King's survey

124. Jack's lock and mill. The mill was probably built by George Cooke about 1800, just after the canal cut was dug.

125. *Mr Ashby's fishing house stood on an island in the River Colne, which is now in the grounds of Black Jack's restaurant*

126. *The original lock house at Jack's lock was built in 1799 and is shown in the centre of the picture near the bridge. The lock-keeper received 15 shillings a week wages. A new lock house was built on the further side of the bridge about 1914. The cottage on the left is Eversden, with only a small amount of its timber frame showing. Nowadays it is called Black Jack's Cottage and having acquired a thatched roof, looks quite different.*

of 1699 shows Eversden on the east bank of the stream, but no other buildings. Rocque's map of Middlesex dated 1754 gives a similar picture, with the Colney Stream running off to join the River Colne, leaving an island where the restaurant and gardens are now. A plan on one of the canal deeds dated 1797 names Eversden as Branches Farm and shows a small building on the island. It is probably the little brick hut that stands in the present gardens and was a "fishing house" when William Ashby owned Eversden and the fishery in the river. George Cooke seems to have erected the new mill on the island, while the new cut for the canal was being dug. A Canal Company Minute Book mentions "a mill erected at Harefield with a cut made thereto from the canal without any previous application having been made to the Company for their consent thereto".

Throughout the nineteenth century it ground corn and was called Jack's Mill. It was leased with the coppermills to the Mines Royal Company and later to Mr Newell. Edward and Robert Hoyer Millar took out a 21-year-lease in 1896, and started grinding sawdust to produce a powder used in the manufacture of linoleum (Troy Mill was used for the same purpose at the same time) but the mill went out of business about 1906 and became a private house. The Billyard-Leakes lived there for a time during the First World War and Mr O.B. Howell was resident after the Second World War. The restaurant is part of the building once known as The Lodge. 'Black' Jack's is first used in a canal document early this century, but only came into general use much later.

THE GRAND JUNCTION CANAL

The Grand Junction Canal was intended to improve communications between London and Birmingham, by linking the Thames with the Oxford Canal at Braunston. The route proposed in October 1792 ran through Harefield and joined the Thames at Brentford. The narrow strip of land to be purchased by the Canal Company, running through Cow Moor and Harefield Moor was valued in the summer of 1795 by Richard Cooper of Denham, a land surveyor. Letters flew between the Company's Commissioners and Sir Roger Newdigate who was concerned about his interests. George Cooke was happy with the £221 19s ¾d he received for just over three acres along the bottom of his park and Mrs Elizabeth Partridge accepted £99 7s 6d for about one acre near Gulchwell.[3]

The section of the canal that went through Harefield opened in September 1797. From Gulchwell south, it mainly flowed in the bed of the Colney Stream as far as the Flakes where the Coppermill stream ran off creating an island, across which the lock was cut. From Jack's Mill a new water course was created, carried by aqueduct across the Frays River, so that

127. Moorhall bridge in 1934. The Halfway House (half-way between Harefield and Denham) was rebuilt a few years later and has been renamed the Horse & Barge. The bay-windowed house on the left still stands, but is well below the level of the present road, which was built when the bridge was widened.

128. A page from an early nineteenth-century canal clerk's pocket book, referring to carriage of sea-coal to London and the back carriage of dung and manure.

water would not be drawn from the Frays to the detriment of local milling interests. A lock was built at Gulchwell. A brick bridge carried the diverted lane across to Draytonford and Maple Cross and there was a lock and a swing bridge at Coppermills carrying the road to West Hyde and the Chalfonts. The next lock and brick bridge were beside Eversden and there was a swing bridge at Broadwater Farm (the new cut was driven through its rickyard); a lock and brick bridge at Moorhall, and one more bridge in Harefield parish before Denham Deep Lock was reached.

The canal carried a great many goods straight through Harefield to London, but wharves were soon built south of Coppermills and at Moorhall, where goods could be landed. A pocket book that probably belonged to an early nineteenth-century clerk shows the variety of goods carried on the canal: coke, beer, bricks, wheat, flour, wood, bran, coals, ashes, barley, malt, oats, beans, salt, pantiles, soot, Russia Tallow, lime, hay and straw. Waste materials like soot and ashes were loaded onto the empty boats in London and used as manure and by brickmakers in the countryside. In the 1860s Charles Newdigate-Newdegate was landing coal from his own mine, Griff Colliery in Warwickshire, at Moorhall and taking back hay.

Although the canal gave a fillip to the development of industry in Harefield by providing cheap transport, thus increasing the choice of employment available to labourers, it did not in itself employ many local people. The 1861 census records only two canal boatmen, one living at Hill End and the other in the High Street, a barge carter and two barge loaders. This was probably because by the 1830s the narrow boats were mainly worked by families who lived on the water and were constantly mobile and stayed on the canal from one generation to the next. Much concern was expressed later in the century about the lack of schooling for the boat children.

There were accidents. Joseph Kempster aged seven, a boatman's son, was drowned in 1888. The water was only four feet deep, but his feet had stuck in the mud. More happily in 1892, young Charles Dixon and his horse were rescued from the canal near the Fisheries public house opposite the coppermills. The local paper was in moralising mood. "Young lads drive at what speed they please! Cannot they be compelled to lead their horses by the head at a spot like this where the slightest hitch means falling into the canal?"

129. A general view of the mills in the mid-twentieth century. The River Colne flows across the bottom of the photograph behind the lock house and the Fisheries Inn. Coppermill lock was cut across an island in the Colne created by the mill stream. The oldest part of the mills and Mines Royal House are toward the right hand side of the illustration. In the centre, a row of workers' cottages fronts Summerhouse Lane. Park Works are on the top side of the lane.

130. *United Asbestos Company workers in 1891.*

131. *The belfry at the United Asbestos Company works c.1900. The garden of the Manor House (formerly Mines Royal House) is on the right and the mill stream emerges from under the road bridge on the left.*

COPPERMILLS

Once the canal had been built, the mills were converted from paper making to copper rolling and travellers were soon writing of the "celebrated copper mills".[4] They were a feature of Harefield for eighty years and the name is still current as the name of the lock. Robert George Spedding lived at Mines Royal House (the Manor House) and managed the works, employing 103 people in 1803. Copper ore from the Lake District and Cornwall was taken by sea to smelting works in Glamorgan, then brought to Harefield to be rolled into copper sheets, mainly used for sheathing the bottoms of the Royal Navy's wooden ships to protect them against the depredations of the toredo worm. Two of the buildings being restored and converted into offices in 1995 date from this period.

Workers walked to work from Denham, Mill End and West Hyde as well as Harefield. A few were accommodated in a row of two-up, two-down cottages provided on the canalside opposite the mills. They were satirically known as Workhouse Row because of the poverty of their occupants. An architect rescued them from demolition in the 1960s: some were extended and they now make desirable waterside residences and have been renamed Coppermill Lock. A Grand Junction Canal waymarker outside the end one, says "Braunston 77 miles".

Trade at the mills declined with the introduction of iron ships and only 86 men and boys were employed in 1851 and 72 in 1861. The Mines Royal Company closed down the mills in 1863.

A Major Wieland took out a 60-year lease in 1864, but appears only to have stripped such assets as the copper gutters from the roofs and to have sold off coals, sheet and bar iron and machinery. He sub-let the mills and Manor House to Messrs Walker, Berthon & Delloys in 1868. Mr Delloys had the house redecorated and furnished in handsome style by Mr Dear, a London upholsterer, to whom he owed more than £2000 before the end of the year. Poor Mr Dear lost heavily over the business, because when the case came to court, it was discovered that Mr Delloys had not paid his rent either and the judge allowed Mr Wieland to seize the goods that belonged to Mr Dear in lieu.

PAPER MILLS AGAIN

Mr Thomas Newell of the Rue Martel, Paris, took over the lease and reopened the mills in 1870 to produce high quality paper of the type produced in France, using imported French workmen. Though he was not commercially successful – he went into liquidation in 1879 – his social contribution to the village was significant. He built a lecture room at the mills for the edification of his forty-strong work force, and here he displayed dissolving views for his talk on Paris and he and his wife, who played the organ, put on musical evenings and gave singing lessons. The Newells attended the Baptist church and entertained the Sunday School children at the mills. The pastor, Mr Turner. chaired the lecture meetings.[5]

ASBESTOS MILLS

The United Asbestos Company (*see also illustrations 130 and 131*) next leased the mills from 1882. The asbestos was manufactured from fibre brought from Brentford and cement from Coles and Shadbolt's Cement Works at Broadwater Farm. Asbestos was just coming into commercial use as a result of the Company's efforts and a government contract to supply asbestos packing to the Royal Navy was obtained in 1884. The works prospered. and the manager claimed in a letter to the local paper that the Harefield mills were the biggest in Europe. They certainly employed a lot of local men and women – between 400 and 500 in 1901.

The workers had an exciting day in 1889 when the Staghounds were meeting at Maple Cross. A deer plunged into the canal and swam around in circles before running into the spinning room. When noosed it dragged his captor round the yards until being locked up in the coach house.

In 1909 the Company purchased the mills that they had leased for so long, from Mr Hossack, who had just bought much of the Harefield Park estate, and the next year joined up with Bell's Asbestos Company to become Bell's United Asbestos Company. The sale included the mansion house, with gardens on the south side of the road, 22 workers' cottages, some on Summerhouse Lane and some in the corner of a garden just where the traffic lights at the bottom of Park Lane are today, as well as Workhouse Row.[6]

Trade declined and a strike was called to protest against a proposed rundown in production in 1913, but it picked up during the First World War and the factory expanded into new buildings on the top side of Summerhouse Lane and along the wharves on the south side of Park Lane. One of the new buildings with Swiss-style eaves, was the canteen, reached by an elaborate flight of steps that can still be seen. Fire containers, pipe claddings and brake linings were being manufactured and a product called Poilite. It was made in sheets and roof tiles and house claddings were cut from it. Poilite tiles may be seen on the roofs of houses at Hill End, in Summerhouse Lane and at the top of Park Lane. The work was almost certainly unhealthy as employees remember the air being full of asbestos particles, but no sickness or death was actually attributed to working conditions. There were more than 2000 employees in the 1920s but disaster came with the Depression. The Asbestos Company sold the mills to Turner and Newall in 1929

132. The United Asbestos canteen on the top side of Summerhouse Lane. The steps still exist, but are obstructed by a wartime air-raid shelter. Two hostels of similar size were erected behind the canteen, presumbly to house workers during the First World War.

133. A club for the unemployed was set up in Harefield in the 1930s.

and much unemployment was caused in the village when they were closed down two years later.

Turner & Newall sold all the land south of Summerhouse Lane to Vulcanson's of Guildford in September 1935[7]; land north of Belfry Avenue went to Uxbridge Urban District Council in January 1936[8]; the Hill Factory, Park Lane, was bought by Harry Platts and Frank Platts of Leicester, an engineer and haulage contractor, in February 1936[9]; and the canteen and factory buildings on the north side of Summerhouse Lane were sold to John Alexander Whitehead in 1937[10]

Three rubber companies, Compressed Rubber Products, Superbuilt Products Ltd (formerly the Nibby Truck Company) and Rubberware Ltd came together and opened in the Vulcanson premises in 1935. They became the Harefield Rubber Company in 1963. Rubber flooring, PVC industrial doors and microcellular soling and heat resistant rubber sheets were made. The Rubber Company began to move its operations elsewhere in the 1980s.[11]

Winstone Printing Inks occupied the Platts' site from 1948 and later Croda, an ink and printing roller company came there. This Park Works area is now cleared of buildings and awaiting redevelopment, but the name has been transferred to the old distemper works further along the lane.

The wharf was destroyed by fire on the night of 15th October 1985 at a time when plans to redevelop the whole site were causing local concern. Salamander Wharf, an appropriately named office block, was built on the land nearest the road and Swan Reach, a waterside development of town houses, some with narrow boat moorings, went up along Jack's Lane in the late 1980s and early 1990s. The manager's house (the Manor House) was beautifully restored in 1994 and made into offices, as yet without tenants. The renovation of the early nineteenth-century central mill, is almost complete in 1995. It has been given a new name, 'Royal Quay', a reminder of the Mines Royal Company.

LIME, BRICKS AND CEMENT

Sir George Cooke had several chalk pits on his land near the canal and the Harefield Lime Company opened up before 1802, north of the Summerhouse, where there had been a tumbling bay before the river was made navigable. A side cut, long since filled in, was made from the canal for the works branching off the canal on the north side of Red Cottage.

The Lime Works and four workers' cottages in Summerhouse Lane were let to a Mr Cooper in the 1890s, though the Cooper family may have leased the works for a very long time. In 1868 there was a sad accident there when an overhang on which a man was standing collapsed, bringing down some 70-80 tons of chalk. He was buried up to his knees, but suffered such severe back injuries that he died 45 minutes later. A press report said that he had worked for Mrs Cooper of Hill End, proprietor of the works for 49 years.

The lime works were part of the Harefield Park sale to Mr Hossack in 1908 and were sold on to the Gelatine White Company of Woolwich the next month.[12] By 1934 tramways had been laid into the chalk quarry and distemper was being manufactured. The area occupied by the lime works is now rather confusingly called Park Works and houses a number of small industrial and commercial units.

134. *Workers celebrate the end of the First World War. An Australian soldier from the hospital stands in the midst of the crowd.*

Sir Christopher Baynes established another lime works at Broadwater Farm in the early nineteenth century, with its own cut from the canal, which later belonged to George Robinson, lord of the manor of Ickenham.[13] It lay down the hill at the back of the White Horse and was reached down a track from Church Hill. The increasing overlay of Reading Beds and London Clay that had to be removed to get at the chalk, led in the 1860s to brickmaking as an ancillary activity. The brickfield continued manufacture until the 1920s. Coles & Shadbolt's cement works which supplied the asbestos company started in the same quarry about the same time as United Asbestos came to Harefield. Barges carried the cement the short distance to the mills. The works closed at the same time as the asbestos company. In 1885 wages were 3s 6d a day for clay digging and 5s 6d a day for working the kilns, but the work was hard. It continued seven days a week and men usually only had one weekend off in three.[14] Agricultural labourers at the same period were earning only 16 shillings a week. Cottages for the brickfield workers built in 1916 still stand in Church Hill.

The pits left by these old workings were used as council dumps and during the 1950s, when rubbish from Hammersmith was being deposited there, strong emotions were aroused locally because of the health threat caused by the dust, dirt and flies coming from the refuse tips. In August 1954 a protest march of 120 local people was led down Whitehall by Ernest Bugbee, to deliver a letter at 10 Downing Street. They were accompanied by a piper playing a specially composed lament, and the drummers of the Harefield Boys' Brigade.

135. *The lime works at the end of Summerhouse Lane. The quarry has many interesting chalk plants and is now a Site of Special Scientific Interest.   The cut from the canal can be seen at the side of Red Cottage.*

136. *The brickfield behind the White Horse in Church Hill, where production began as an ancillary activity to the lime works at Broadwater Farm. Coles & Shadbolt's cement works started in the same quarry about 1910.*

137. *These brickfield workers' cottages were built in Church Hill in 1916. The White Horse stands behind its sign and the Almshouses are on the right.*

138. *Protesters against the filling of the old workings with rubbish from Hammersmith, queuing on the green for their special coach tickets (price 3 shillings return!). The Revd Dennis Connor is on the right.*

139. *Maud Field near Bayhurst Wood was the home of Quakers at the beginning of the eighteenth century. This house later became Willow Farm. After the present Willow Farm was built in 1905, the old house was used for storage and eventually demolished.*

Chapels and Churches

QUAKERS[1]

In the late seventeenth century there were four Quaker families in Harefield. Richard Richardson, formerly publican at the George Inn, Uxbridge, where Quaker meetings were held before the present Meeting House was erected in the town in 1692, moved to Bungers Hill (later Greentrees) Farm in 1686. In 1699 Gregory King found him living there with his second wife, his daughter by his first wife, a step-daughter and a servant, Mary Swain. He noted that his tenant, Jeffrey Dennington, another Quaker, with his wife (who had been married before), four children and a maid servant had recently moved to Uxbridge. The wife died there and Jeffrey Dennington returned to Harefield in 1702 to marry Mary Lovett, widow of Thomas Lovett of Breakspears-by-the-Heath, a Quaker friend of his. Scandal was occasioned by his moving into her house although the wedding did not take place until 1704. James Pond, a hoop-shaver from Rickmansworth, lived at Maud Field near Bayhurst Wood after his marriage to Mary Wheeler from a Quaker family of Hill End.

They all suffered mild persecution for their faith, although the manor court ruling of 1692 re church attendance specifically excluded dissenters from the Church of England. The Lovetts were among a group excommunicated by the turbulent minister, Roger Davies in 1678, which had legal implications for them. James Pond and Richard Richardson had goods distrained (four pewter dishes and six sheep) because they refused to contribute to a church rate in 1706. They were, however, overseers of the poor for they believed in serving the community, but not in supporting "a steeple house".

BAPTISTS[2]

A handsome Baptist chapel was built on the Rickmansworth Road in 1834 at the cost of John Bailey, a Quaker from Uxbridge, who wanted to save the youth of Harefield from drunkenness and debauchery on the Sabbath (and presumably other days as well). The numbers attending had risen to 70 in the 1840s, but they fluctuated. Mr Newell of the Paper Mill was a strong Baptist and encouraged them by providing treats for the members of the church during the 1870s. The pastor was then the Revd E. Turner, but like all the other ministers was not resident. After Mr Newell's departure congregations dropped and the chapel closed for a time, to reopen in 1884 in association with chapels in Watford and later Rickmansworth. In the main lay-pastors have looked after the chapel this century.

140. *Harefield Baptist Chapel built in 1834 stands on the right, separated from the Methodist chapel of 1864 by Chapel Row. Only the Baptist chapel still exists.*

METHODISM

Methodism was established in Harefield by Robert Barnes of Harefield Grove. The first services and Sunday School classes were held in his coach house in 1863 and a large crowd of 400 or more were attracted to them, some adults coming principally to learn how to read and write.[3] He built a chapel on the Rickmansworth Road, separated from the Baptist Chapel only by a row of cottages in 1864. According to Mr Vernon's *Notes on the Parish of Harefield* published in 1872, Mr Barnes "built a very pretty chapel, which he afterwards made over to the Wesleyans. There was at that time but one Wesleyan family in the Parish".

Numbers soon increased, perhaps on account of Mr John McCallum who came to manage the asbestos works in 1884 and joined them He was a man of great enthusiasm, especially in musical matters, leading the chapel choir and being a member of the Tonic Solfa Society. Perhaps he was continuing the tradition started at the mills by Mr Newell, with his vocal music classes. The chapel choir sang at Harvest Suppers and Temperance Society and Band of Hope meetings. The Methodists were sufficiently strong in numbers to build a hall in 1906 for which McCallum laid the foundation stone. Numbers declined after the First World War, but were boosted for a time in the 1940s by an influx of evacuees.

Although children were often sent to the Sunday School when they were small because it was nearer than the parish church, they later transferred to St Mary's, perhaps because of Mr Harland, vicar from 1870 to 1920. He was a cheerful man and active in chasing members of his flock who failed to attend church and probably lured a number away from the chapels. The chapel closed and was demolished in 1986. The sheltered housing on the site contains a room for services.

ICKENHAM'S INDEPENDENT CHAPEL

Providence Congregational Chapel was established in Uxbridge in 1777 and attracted members from nearby villages. William Brickett and his wife, who lived in Glebe Lane, attended the meeting house on Lynch Green and in 1831 were encouraged by the deacons to try to form a group in Ickenham.[4] The prayer meetings in their cottage were so popular that a chapel was built in 1835, on waste land on the edge of Ickenham Green next to the Soldier's Return. Three of the deacons of Uxbridge Providence were made trustees and the chapel was built at a cost of £160. It opened on 3rd November 1835 and was served from Uxbridge until 1919. The congregation flourished and a school room was added in 1861. The Brickett family continued their association – William's son, David attended morning service at Uxbridge and afternoon Sunday School and evening service at

141.   *The Brickett cottage in Ickenham, where prayer meetings were held in the early 1830s.*

142.   *The Congregational chapel erected in 1835 on the edge of Ickenham Green. The picture shows it in 1936, when a new church had opened in Swakeleys Road and the site was for sale.*

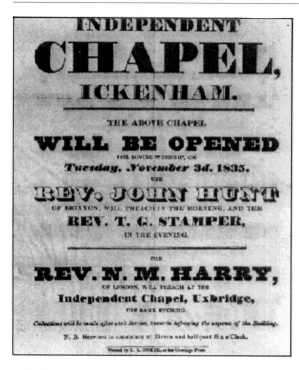

Ickenham. He grew up to be a prominent member of the church and community and was on the first parish council in 1894.[5]

A hall was built at the back of the chapel in 1921, but building on the Swakeleys estate in the 1920s increased numbers to such an extent that the village hall was hired for services in 1930. A new church in contemporary style was opened in 1936 in Swakeleys Road on a corner of the old rectory field and next door to the new rectory. It is now, like all Congregational churches, the United Reformed Church and continues to flourish.

The old chapel still stands on Ickenham High Road right on the edge of the canal feeder, now used by Saich & Edwards as a store place and wood yard.

ROMAN CATHOLICISM

Very few references to Roman Catholics in either Ickenham or Harefield occur. Bernard Brocas of Swakeleys was fined for not attending St Giles in 1584 and Elizabeth Waters for the same thing on several occasions between 1593-7, but later rectors reported no known papists in the parish. Until the Gilbeys leased Swakeleys in late Victorian and Edwardian times catholics are never mentioned. Sarah Shorediche of Cawderstones, Berwick-on-Tweed, writing to her

143. The notice announcing the opening of the new chapel in November 1835.

144. A painting of the interior of the old candle-lit chapel.

nephew in 1950, said that she stayed in Ickenham in 1895 and wept over the condition of the church, putting it down to the fact that "the Gilbeys were RCs, so would have no interest in a protestant church".[6] When the Sacred Heart church was established in Ruislip in 1920, the catholic parish included Ickenham and still extends as far as Swakeleys Road. The rest of Ickenham is in the catholic parish of St Bernadette's, Hillingdon.

The Revd Reginald B. Fellows MA was a convert to Catholicism and having been a stockbroker before entering the priesthood had money of his own. He built St Matthew's catholic church, Northwood in 1922-3, where he became first parish priest. Foreseeing the need for a church in Harefield at a future date, he purchased a site in the vicarage garden in 1929. It remained empty for many years and in the 1950s priests from Ruislip said mass in the British Legion hall. Not until the Revd Lionel Keane came to Harefield in March 1963 was anything done about providing a church. He moved into a house in Dunster Close (bought by the Westminster diocese six months earlier) and converted the garage into a small chapel. Helped by the skills and enthusiasm of his parishioners and the other villagers, he erected a hall-church on what had become Merle Avenue, which was opened by Cardinal Heenan in 1965. This large building was available for use by all kinds of functions from Bingo to wedding receptions (the altar was curtained off) and was used by the school

146. The new Congregational church in 1936.

and AQD for prize-giving ceremonies. There was a great spirit of ecumenism in Harefield and the Revd Dennis Connor of St Mary's and Father Keane worked together. The church's dedication to St Paul of the Nations symbolised the church's outward-looking attitude arising from the Vatican Council of 1961. Later priests (Fr Keane retired in 1976) have built a sanctuary onto the church.[7]

145. St Paul's Roman Catholic church, Harefield. This hall-church was opened in Merle Avenue in 1965.

147. Harefield School built c.1858. St Mary's church hall now stands on the site.

Village Schools

HAREFIELD

Responsibility for teaching the poorer children of Harefield seems to have been undertaken by the minister from the late sixteenth century. In the seventeenth century resident clergymen were paid small sums by the lords of the manor to perform this duty, probably at the Almshouses, where Sir Richard Newdigate provided a special room for the school in 1692. Perhaps the administration broke down because in 1700 he had a list drawn up of the names and ages of all the children in the parish together with their parents' circumstances, intending to "be so very kind as to have them taught to read and instructed in the Principles of Religion". By 1728 the 'Charity' School provided clothing and lessons for ten boys and ten girls. Sir Roger Newdigate mentions visiting the school in his diary for 1794, when he gave the master 2s 6d and 1s 6d to each child.[1]

A "commodious schoolroom" was built on the waste on the east side of the High Street, by public subscription about 1813, when John Penrose, one of the subscribers was minister. Eighty boys and sixty girls attended the 'free school' in the 1840s, although some at least seem to have paid 2d a week. The land on which the schoolroom stood was given to the parish in 1858 by John Penrose who had left Harefield in 1814, but was the sole surviving subscriber and Sir Charles Newdegate-Newdigate gave an adjoining field to serve as a playground. The school was reorganised as a Church of England school with Sir Charles having right of appointment and dismissal of staff. It may have been rebuilt at this time, but accommodation remained very simple. In 1871 a single room divided by movable screens served more than 100 boys, girls and infants, presided over by Mr and Mrs C.J. Robertson and a pupil-teacher. The master's house was next door.[2]

Overcrowding was eased when the infants went off to a separate school in 1871 and another schoolroom was added in 1879. Samuel Blud, master from 1887, had the reputation of being "a bit of a terror". He was still in charge when the Middlesex County Council built a new school which opened in 1907 on land on the south side of Park Lane, bought from the Vernons. The old school, which continued to be used for Sunday School was demolished in 1972 and replaced with a church hall. The new school was being considered a little old fashioned by the 1980s and was completely rebuilt in 1989.

148. Mr Samuel Blud with a class at Harefield School in 1904.

THE INFANTS' SCHOOL[3]

The infants' school opened in May 1871 in a room in the Memorial Hall at the corner of Hill End and Rickmansworth Roads, a building erected by Robert Barnes of Harefield Grove in memory of his son who had died while a student at Oxford in 1864. When Mr Barnes sold Harefield Grove in 1868 he offered to make over the hall to trustees, but his offer was declined and the hall fell into disuse. He died soon afterwards. Mr Harland, the newly appointed vicar, seeing the need for an infants' school, obtained permission from Miss Barnes to establish one there, under his own superintendence and quite distinct from the Church of England School in the High Street.

The first teacher, Miss Caroline Labram opened the school and qualified for her government certificate within a few months, thus attracting a government grant. Assisted by a monitoress and a pupil-teacher, she coped with sixty children and Mr Harland faithfully visited the school twice a week for the whole 36 years of its existence. The ladies from the gentry houses were also regular visitors, assisting the staff in the teaching of needlework and encouraging the children. In November 1871 "Miss Vernon visited and read letters the children had written. She appeared very pleased." Miss Sawyer of Harefield (now Sydenham) Lodge and Miss Bunion called at 4 o'clock one Friday afternoon in July 1876 "to hear the children sing. Kept children 20 minutes after time. Both ladies were highly amused and very pleased with the singing." This encroachment on free time seems a little thoughtless, but Miss Sawyer was one of the ladies, along with Mrs Byles of Harefield House and the Misses Vernon of Harefield Park, who paid the school pence of some of the poorer children.

The infants' school generally received favourable comments from government inspectors. "This is a good specimen of a village Infants' School. The children appear happy and well cared for, and the elements of instruction are successfully taught. The discipline is good", ran the report in 1874. But in 1876 the inspector noted copying and warned that this would mean sacrificing the grant if it happened again. The infants moved to the new council school in 1907.

149. *Standard VI and VII outside the new Harefield School.*

150. *The Memorial Hall by Harefield Green, which was used as an infants' school from 1871 to 1907.*

151. *Harefield High Street in the early years of this century. The end of Harefield School can be seen with the tall, gabled teacher's house beside it.*

152. Sydenham Lodge in Rickmansworth Road, home of the Sawyers in the 1870s. It is now an annex to the hospital.

ICKENHAM

There was a charity school in Ickenham in 1819, run on Lancasterian lines (in which, under supervision, older children taught younger children) and providing clothing as well as education to fifty pupils, but nothing is known of its whereabouts. Thereafter the Clarkes of Swakeleys seem to have provided educational facilities in the village. Thomas Truesdale Clarke founded a Church of England school in 1823 and there were ten boys and twenty girls attending, paying school pence at the time of the government enquiry prior to the 1833 Education Act.[4] There was a Dame School at Home Farm in 1846. Miss Ann Wilson, a schoolmistress who was living at Home Farm in 1861, however, was probably teaching at the Charity School.

A new school and house was built on waste land on the corner of Ickenham High Road and Austins Lane in 1866, perhaps replacing the old building. Miss Ann Wilson was in charge. The money for the schoolhouse was raised by public subscription, led by the second Thomas Truesdale Clarke, who owned the land on which it was built and the school itself. It was financed by a combination of subscriptions and small fees, but Mr Clarke made up any shortfall. Children who gained certificates of merit had their school pence returned to them as a reward.

The school was inspected in 1873 and a log book kept thereafter. Miss Wilson was assisted by two monitoresses, who worked alternate weeks. Helen Clarke, the unmarried daughter of Thomas Truesdale Clarke, then in her forties, effectively ran the school. She regularly took reading and dictation, appointed new teachers, gave out prizes and organised an annual tea for the children at Swakeleys. The children sang in concerts which she arranged in aid of the church organ fund. The rector and his wife, Mr and Mrs Beauchamp Pell were also active visitors.[5]

153. An early photograph of Ickenham School 1866-1934, on the corner of Ickenham High Road and Austins Lane.

Early Inspectors' reports were not good. In 1876 children were "tidy and well mannered but the attainments are sadly defective, especially in arithmetic....the infants'....instruction is almost entirely wanting". It was after this report that the first reference to teaching arithmetic appears in the log book.

When the Great Western & Great Central Railway line was being built across Ickenham Green after 1900, village parents objected to the "rough" children of the navvies attending the school. They lived in tents on the green and for a time a Dame School was set up for them in one of the farmhouses, probably Beatonswood.[6]

The school was beginning to be overcrowded in the 1920s and it stood on the edge of a fairly narrow road in the way of the increasing traffic. The older children moved into the village hall, known as Ickenham Temporary Council School in 1928 and when the old building was demolished for road widening in 1929 the infants went to the village hall and the rest to a new council school built in Long Lane, just outside the parish. The old village school was finally replaced by Breakspear Primary School in Bushey Road in 1937. Glebe Primary was built in 1952 to serve the population on the further side of Ickenham High Road.

154. Breakspear Primary School in Bushey Road. It was opened in 1937.

ABSENTEEISM

At both Ickenham and Harefield absences were noted with concern in log books as school grants in some measure depended upon attendance. Serious illnesses like diphtheria and scarlet fever occurred and occasionally children died. Minor medical conditions associated with malnutrition, such as bad eyes, eruptions on the head and itch were common, as were chilblains in the winter. Hard weather kept many children at home at a time when there was little waterproof clothing and children walked long distances. Holidays were not so long as today and the timing of the summer break depended upon local haymaking and harvest, when the children helped in the fields, so it is not surprising that time was taken off for treats such as fairs and May Day, or to follow the hounds when the hunt came to the villages.

The need for children to contribute to the household economy was another potent reason for absence. "The acorns still seem to be the cause of many children not attending school. I have seen the attendance officer, he says it is useless taking them to court as the Magistrates will not convict, and in cases where they do, the fine is so small, usually 1 shilling or 1s 6d that they do not mind". The acorns were sold to local farmers at the rate of one shilling the bushel, to feed pigs and sheep. Mushrooms were gathered too. One enterprising boy from the Shrubs used to get up early, gather the mushrooms, then tramp round all the greengrocers' shops in Rickmansworth, selling them at 3d a pound. His mother bought his shoes and suits with the money. Beating at shoots was very popular with boys, for the money received was good and a meal was given at mid-day. There was a general feeling that "there was no such thing as going to school if you could earn a bob at that time of day"

SECONDARY SCHOOLS

Harefield Parish Council agreed to pay £147 10s towards the cost of a County Secondary School in the Greenway, Uxbridge in 1907, whither such children as sought further education went. There was no secondary school in Harefield until John Penrose School, opened in 1954, named after the minister who had been involved with the charity school. Because of the rural surroundings the school teaches agriculture as well as general subjects. It became comprehensive in 1977 along with all other secondary schools in the Borough of Hillingdon.

DOUAY MARTYRS SCHOOL

A Roman Catholic Secondary Modern School opened in Edinburgh Drive, Ickenham in 1962. It has greatly expanded in recent years and now serves the Roman Catholic population for the whole of the Borough of Hillingdon.

PRIVATE SCHOOLS

There have been few private schools in the area. The Revd. Edward Barnard ran one in Harefield Grove in 1804, but nothing else about it is known.

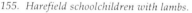

155. Harefield schoolchildren with lambs.

156 and 157. A Harefield sports day

VYNER'S SCHOOL

This school in Warren Road, strictly speaking is on the Hillingdon side of the parish boundary. It opened as a grammar school in 1969 and is named after Sir Robert Vyner who lived at Swakeleys in Charles II's time.

ICKENHAM HIGH SCHOOL FOR GIRLS

This school flourished from 1925 until 1961. It catered for girls between the ages of four and seventeen and had a few small boys who received preparatory education. From 1927 it was situated in the old Rectory in Swakeleys Road. After it closed down, the house was demolished and Eleanor Grove stands on the site.

158. *Mr Kingsnorth, butler at Swakeleys, was described as both butler and grocer in the 1861 census and he and his wife were running the shop shown on the left-hand side of this photograph, beside Ickenham pond. Ten years later his son-in-law, Ebenezer Hall, was a baker here. By 1881 the shop had become the Post Office, with William Weedon as postmaster. It lives on in popular memory as Miss Butler's shop, for she was postmistress from 1903 to 1939.*

Village Life

GETTING ABOUT

The life of the agricultural labourers and mill workers of Ickenham and Harefield was centred in the villages where they lived because transport was scarce and working hours were long. Journeys elsewhere were usually undertaken on foot, with occasional trips on the carrier's cart when there was money to spare. In the 1890s, Mr Jefferies, the Harefield carrier, went to Uxbridge and Rickmansworth on alternate days charging a return fare to Uxbridge of 6d. Several innkeepers like Thomas Miller of the King's Arms advertised themselves as 'Fly Proprietors' and hired out·vehicles. His brake carried seven people, three on each side and one outside and the charge was 1s 6d per person to Northwood Station. Organised outings to places like Ascot and the Derby, or to Hampton Court travelled by brake. The Metropolitan Railway came to Northwood and Rickmansworth in 1887 and young men from Harefield sometimes walked to Rickmansworth to catch a train to Watford. In some ways Ickenham was less isolated than Harefield being within easier walking distance (two miles) of Uxbridge and at the beginning of this century two stations were built near the village. Ickenham Halt on the Metropolitan line to Uxbridge opened in September 1905 and West Ruislip (then called Ruislip and Ickenham) on the Great Central and Great Western Railway line in 1906.

The isolation and frequent statements in reminiscences that no one travelled very far, is belied to a certain extent by the fact that 44% of the people living in Harefield at the time of the 1881 census had been born elsewhere (14.3% in London and other parts of Middlesex; 15% in Bucks/Herts; 14.7% further afield). More than half of the females were incomers. They made up for the young women in the 15-19 year-old age group, who left Harefield to go into service elsewhere. They had probably moved there to work at the mills or as servants at the big houses. A similar pattern emerges in Ickenham where 40.9% of the population had been born elsewhere in 1841 (20% from other counties). The majority of the servants in the great houses were incomers and only the higher servants like Mr Kingsnorth the butler at Swakeleys stayed from one census to the next. In other fields those with responsible positions like farm bailiffs, farmers, foremen and with skilled jobs such as carpenters, came from outside, whereas the more lowly labouring jobs were filled by natives. In the industrial services sector in Harefield in 1881, 56.5% of the labourers were locally born, but all the clerks were from other places. In agriculture, which was the major employer, 69.5% of agricultural labourers were from Harefield, but 70.6% of the farmers were immigrants. People moved away for the sake of getting on in life.

159. *A brake standing outside the Cricketers in Harefield High Street about 1907. The inn was advertising a tea-garden for visiting trippers. Carrick & Coles was an Uxbridge department store.*

160. Next door to Ickenham post office stood this interesting timber-framed cottage, with brick nogging infill in herringbone pattern. The Hibbert family lived there from the time of the 1841 census. In 1887 it was replaced by Jubilee Cottage and the Hibberts continued to live there until the 1980s. The cottage and shops facing the pond are all now used as offices.

MEMORIAL HALLS AND INSTITUTES

Many of the social activities in both villages were sponsored by the families living in the big houses and were aimed at improvement through enjoyment. Rooms big enough for large groups to meet in Harefield were available at the Memorial Hall, the Breakspear Institute and at the mills. The Memorial Hall, built to commemorate Robert Barnes's only son who had died while a student at Oxford, was opened in 1864 and stood on the corner of Hill End and Rickmansworth Roads. A reading-room on the ground floor, furnished with newspapers and periodicals and a lecture room upstairs were provided for the use of all parishioners. Mr Barnes financed the running expenses and allowed the hall to be used for all kinds of village activities. The three churches used it for missionary meetings, anniversary celebrations and Sunday School Treats. The children at one of these assemblies were addressed by Mr Barnes who told them that it was "for the improvement of their minds and the uplifting of their souls". Penny Readings and Benevolent Entertainments took place

161. *Harefield Memorial Hall with Chapel Row and the Methodist chapel on the right.*

162. *The Breakspear Institute, built in 1896 by Commander Tarleton. A horse-drawn vehicle approaches along Rickmansworth Road.*

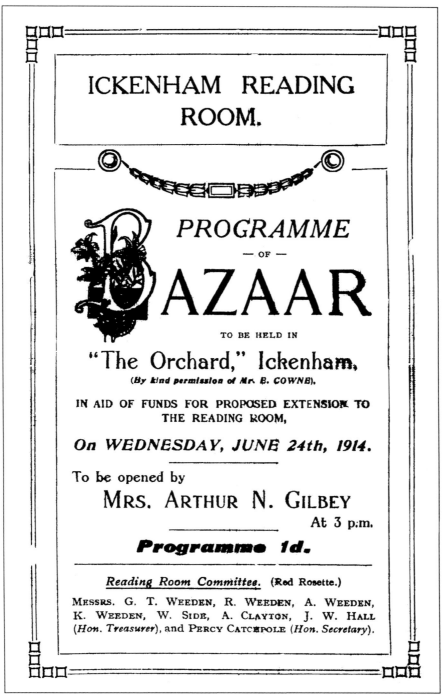

ICKENHAM READING ROOM.

PROGRAMME

— OF —

BAZAAR

TO BE HELD IN

"The Orchard," Ickenham,

(By kind permission of Mr. B. COWNE).

IN AID OF FUNDS FOR PROPOSED EXTENSION TO
THE READING ROOM,

On **WEDNESDAY, JUNE 24th, 1914.**

To be opened by

MRS. ARTHUR N. GILBEY

At 3 p.m.

Programme 1d.

Reading Room Committee. (Red Rosette.)

MESSRS. G. T. WEEDEN, R. WEEDEN, A. WEEDEN,
K. WEEDEN, W. SIDE, A. CLAYTON, J. W. HALL
(*Hon. Treasurer*), and PERCY CATCHPOLE (*Hon. Secretary*).

163. *Programme of a bazaar, held in 1914, to raise funds to extend Ickenham Reading Room
(also known as the Men's Institute). The extension was built after the war as a memorial to those
who had died.*

164. *Mothers and babies on Harefield Green on Welfare Day about 1930.*

there, raising money for such worthy objects as providing flannel for petticoats for twenty widows, as well as more formal lectures. Mr T. Smith's 'Curiousities of Chemistry' was very well attended in 1868.

Although the Infants' School used the hall during the day from 1871 to 1907, lectures and other activities continued in the evenings. Vestry Meetings and Parish Meetings were held there at the turn of the century. Middlesex County Council maternity and child welfare clinic met there during the 1930s, and it was used for civil defence during the Second World War. The building was demolished in 1979.

Mr Tarleton's Breakspear Institute, founded in 1896 and built on Rickmansworth Road close to the edge of the Green, was run as a Working Men's Club and provided a hall for concerts, lectures and meetings. Similar activities had been available at the paper mills in Thomas Newell's time and the asbestos works had a string and brass band under the musical Mr McCallum.

In Ickenham lantern slide lectures and similar events took place at the school and occasionally at Swakeleys. The Men's Institute in the High Road was available for billiards, darts and card games, and whist drives and social evenings were fortnightly events at the beginning of this century. The building was extended in memory of those who had died in the First World War and renamed the Memorial Hall. In the early 1920s, Mrs Langton the rector's wife ran a girl's club in one of the rooms and understandingly allowed the boys in for an hour's dancing at the end of the evening. The Memorial Hall, a corrugated iron building, was demolished in 1979 to make way for Lynx House, an office block. The Village Hall was designed by Clifton Davy and built in Swakeleys Road in 1926, the money being raised by the sale of the old school buildings. It opened on the 8th January 1927 and, having a stage and dressing rooms, provided a decent venue for dramatic performances.

SOCIETIES[1]

Temperance groups were well to the fore in the nineteenth century with a Harefield Temperance Society taking over from the Band of Hope in 1886. Meetings of general interest were followed by stirring addresses on the evils of drink and the singing of temperance songs. Mr McCallum obliged with *Three acres and a cow*, which could be achieved by agricultural labourers who practised thrift and eschewed strong drink! The Harefield Choral Society sang at temperance concerts too.

Horticulture was considered an ideal occupation for the workers, as it helped them to feed their families cheaply and discouraged idleness. The Harefield, Ickenham and Ruislip Horticultural Society was

165. A group of slightly reluctant looking recruits to the Pioneer Mission on Harefield Green about 1920.

founded in the 1880s and the first show was held at Breakspears in 1885.

Ickenham had a debating society after the First World War, started by the rector and for male parishioners over the age of fourteen only. Women generally were assumed to have plenty of opportunity to air their views at the Mothers' Union. A Girls' Club was run by the energetic Mrs Langton.

PUBS

Despite the jolly sing-songs and attractions of the institutes, the pubs were the places most frequented by the working men of Ickenham and Harefield. Ickenham gained two new beerhouses, the Soldier's Return and the Fox and Geese, in the nineteenth century, both built on roadside waste. The Soldier's Return was erected in 1828, originally as a cottage and blacksmith's shop. By 1850 Mrs Filkins was running a beershop there and the blacksmith had moved to the Fox and Geese. (Two years earlier a blacksmith called Charles James Filkins had taken over the beerhouse known as the Prince of Wales – now the Prince Hotel – in Harefield.) The unusual name, the Soldier's Return, may come from the comic opera by Theodore Hook (1788-1841). Thomas Montague was both landlord of the Fox and Geese and a blacksmith and his son, William was still the blacksmith in 1902. A few years later Llewellyn

166. The Soldier's Return at Ickenham Green was built in 1828 as a cottage and blacksmith's shop. It had become Mrs Filkins' beerhouse by 1850.

167. When this photograph was taken in the early years of this century, William Clarke was the licensee of the Fox & Geese on Ickenham High Road and Mr Montague, shown with his tools in his hands, was the smith.

168. The White Horse in Church Hill, Harefield, was once two cottages. One part was already a beerhouse by 1699.

No. 311.

ENGLAND AND IRELAND.

Publican's Licence.

6 Geo. 4, c. 81 ; 43 & 44 Vict., c. 20.

No. *641*   No. */v*

Hammersmith   Collection.

I, the undersigned, duly authorized by the Commissioners of Inland Revenue, hereby grant Licence to ~~*Emma Saich*~~ *Thomas Edwy Tinker* residing in a house situate at *Ickenham*, in the Parish of *Ickenham* in the *County* of *Middlesex* and known by the sign of *"Coach & Horses"* to exercise and carry on the Trade or Business of a RETAILER of SPIRITS in the said house, and TO SELL BY RETAIL therein, SPIRITS, WINE, SWEETS, MADE WINES, MEAD, METHEGLIN, BEER, CYDER, and PERRY, to be consumed either on or off the premises, from the day of the date hereof, until and including the Tenth day of October next ensuing, such house and premises being rented or valued at the rent or annual sum of £ *24* , and I also hereby grant Licence to him to deal in and ~~sell~~ TOBACCO and SNUFF during the term above mentioned, he having paid for this Licence, being (a) *an ordinary* Licence, the undermentioned Duties, amounting together to the sum of £ *11 -8 - 3*

Wood moved the smithy again, to the barn (now demolished) beside the Coach & Horses.

The Coach & Horses was licensed by 1759, but the house is much older, being timber framed and dating in part from the sixteenth century. It was the venue for manor courts in the nineteenth century, the last one being held in 1878. The inn was owned by Salter's the Rickmansworth brewers (later taken over by Cannons Brewery).

The King's Arms at Harefield crossroads was simply a house called Baldwins at the Butts in the sixteenth century (presumably the archery butts were set up on the common about here). It was already an inn in 1639 and was known by its present name in the 1690s. An inquest was held on a soldier who had died there in 1696 and William Iley was paid £1 for supplying beer to the jury. Part of the White Horse in Church Hill was Widow Baldwin's alehouse at the same time, but the name is not mentioned until 1744. Gregory King noted an ale house at Hill End in 1699, later called the Plough, near, but not on the site of the modern Plough. Other small ale houses came and went over the years and there were fourteen in Victorian times.

Salter's took over the White Horse in 1779 and Harman's of Uxbridge bought the Cricketers in 1880, but Harefield had its own brewery in Park Lane. It was owned by the Vernons and leased to James Ratcliffe. The malt house stood opposite the green

169. Emma Saich's licence for the Coach & Horses.

170. The Plough, Hill End, Harefield, can be seen on the right about 1920. In the centre of the picture stands the Vernon Arms, named after Mr Vernon of Harefield Park.

171. Tipper Hill, seen from Austins Lane, one of the coverts planted by Mr Clarke of Swakeleys.

near the end of Breakspear Road, an attraction for children coming out of school on the one day a week when the windows were opened. Mr Ratcliffe still leased the brewery house in 1908, but the brewery and malthouse had ceased functioning. Walter Brock bought the house in 1909 and renamed it Foley House, but it has since been demolished. Mr Winship, blacksmith by the King's Arms, built the house called Old Brewery Orchard on the adjoining land.

HUNTING AND SHOOTING

Much enjoyment and some profit was derived by the villagers from following the sporting activities of the families of the great houses. Whenever hounds met in the vicinity children abandoned school to watch and some men and boys followed on foot. The Royal Buckhounds often met at Uxbridge, where deer carted from Windsor were let loose and there were lively runs through Harefield, Ickenham and the surrounding country. A deer that ran through the main streets of Uxbridge was finally captured in the grounds of Swakeleys in 1828 after a disappointingly short run. Thomas Truesdale Clarke's brother-in-law, George Hawkins, who lived at Buntings, joined in a violent attack upon a farmer who had trapped a stag in his barn, near Harrow and would not let it out to continue the run. The farmer subsequently was awarded

damages of £100. Farmers who were generally hostile to the hunt were promised opportunities of coursing and given gifts of venison or tickets to Ascot to appease them for the damage done to hedges and crops. The Old Berkeley and Hertfordshire Fox-hounds were also to be seen in the area.

Shooting parties were held at all the great houses and local men and boys were employed as beaters. The Swakeleys shoots always made their way to Gutteridge Wood by mid-day. Lunch, served by a footman from the house, was taken in a wooden hut in Rough Field next to the wood. An annual 'Farmers' shoot' was held at Swakeleys to which all the tenants were invited.

The game birds and small animals that abounded on the estates were a great temptation and poaching was a popular pastime. John Cooper was caught red handed by Mr Carly, the gamekeeper at Breakspears, in 1868, when he put his hand through a hedge to empty one of seven illegal snares previously set by himself and a friend. "John, I've caught you" said Mr Carly. "Yes, and its a fair catch, too" was the reply. Not all predators, however were human and in 1915 the Swakeleys gamekeeper, Dicky Stent, trapped a golden eagle (surely an escape) that had been attacking his young birds around the hatchery in Gutteridge Wood. Arthur Gilbey, tenant of Swakeleys, presented it to Regent's Park Zoo.

172. *A Harefield football team of the 1930s.*

CRICKET AND FOOTBALL

A public house in Harefield, once called the Bull and Butcher, changed its name to the Cricket Players in 1780, which suggests that the game was already being played in the village. A cricketing story which probably relates to Harefield is recounted in *Double Century*, edited by Marcus Williams. Two gentlemen

The game was extremely popular in Victorian and Edwardian times with the Victoria Cricket Club based at the Memorial Hall from 1863, works teams and scratch teams knocked together by the Billyard-Leakes. In 1923 Mr Avray-Tipping gave the pitch which is still used, out of his gardens at Harefield House. Meals were eaten in local pubs after matches and the cricket club had an annual dinner, held at the King's Arms in 1888 and presided over by Mr Byles. Ickenham fielded a team and played home matches on ground attached to Orchard Cottage where Ivy House Road is now. The club moved in the wake of suburban development, first to the Rectory field about 1920 and then to the present pitch at the end of Oak Avenue. There was another team for a while before the Second World War known as the Ickenham Exiles. When the rector, Mr Carmichael, became captain it was renamed Ickenham St Giles.

The Breakspear Institute had a football club in the 1890s, but Ickenham had too few young men for a team and joined with Ruislip to form Kingsend United, associated with the White Bear pub.

FAIRS AND GYPSIES

Fairs were held in villages all around Middlesex in Victorian times. One or two, like Pinner Fair and Hillingdon, have survived to this day. Ickenham had two, a cattle fair in April and a funfair around Whitsuntide. The funfair continued until 1936 when no stalls were erected on the grass verges in the centre of the village and the right was forfeited. Some activities, like climbing a greasy pole and a women's race for a greased pig, were organised by locals, with prizes being given by the gentry, but most of the stallholders were gypsies

Three gypsies who became involved in a desperate affray at the Lord Nelson beerhouse in Harefield, at the end of July 1840 had been at Harefield Fair the previous Monday, "very busy with dice tables, thimble-rigging etc".[2] They nearly killed R. Collet, Mr Spedding's groom by kicking him in the head, before catching up with a band of five other gypsies, three of them women. A hue and cry ensued led by Constable Atkins and two of the gypsies were captured, but only after one of them called James Map had bitten lumps of flesh out of the constable's hand and thigh. They were lodged at the White Horse for the night, before being conveyed, tied in a cart, to the magistrates and thence committed to the New Prison at Clerkenwell to await trial. The other gypsies escaped but were seen at Colnbrook Fair the following Friday, whither they were pursued by the resilient Constable Atkins.

of Middlesex challenged Francis Trumper and his sheepdog to a match in 1827, a time when gambling on a game's outcome was common. The odds started at five to one against Mr Trumper and his canine team, but the dog fielded the ball so rapidly that the two gentlemen had no time to run between the wickets and the odds changed to four to one on.

The Changing Scene

RAILWAYS ACTUAL AND PROJECTED

In many parts of Middlesex, Northwood 1887 and Ruislip 1904 for instance, suburban development began or was at least planned as soon as railway stations brought the areas within easy reach of town, because large landowners were prepared or even eager to dispose of their land for building. This did not happen in Ickenham and Harefield.

Although Randolf Clarke-Thornhill sold a strip of land running across Ickenham Green to the Great Western & Great Central Joint Committee in 1900 and more land to the Metropolitan Railway, he seems to have had no thoughts of developing his 1400-acre Swakeleys estate. Ickenham Parish Council had to press hard to have a Metropolitan station considered for the farmlands of Ickenham as little revenue was likely, but a small halt opened on 25 September 1905, near Glebe Farm. Ruislip & Ickenham Station (now West Ruislip) followed on the other line, just on the Ruislip side of the parish boundary, on 2 April 1906. Although they made travel to London easier and were crucial to future growth, the stations seem to

174. Mr Cowne provided teas for railway trippers in the garden of Orchard Cottage. It was demolished in 1935 and Ickenham Library now stands on the site.

173. Ickenham Station in Glebe Avenue.

have had little immediate effect upon the parish, other than to bring in day-trippers in search of rural simplicity. Orchard Cottage, on the site of the library, served teas and some villagers sold bunches of flowers from their cottage gardens. The population of 329 in 1901 had only risen to 443 by 1921 and a handful of houses had been built at the bottom of Glebe Avenue.

175. Longwood, Harefield Place, is an example of the type of house built in the grounds of the mansion. It was designed by R. Theodore Beck for Mrs Warren and was featured in the magazine, Ideal Home, in 1946.

SOUTH HAREFIELD HALT[1]

The Great Western & Great Central Joint Committee line having left Ickenham Green, crossed the southern end of Harefield parish near Brackenbury to a station at Denham en route to High Wycombe. A branch line was constructed from the east side of the canal to the lower end of Uxbridge High Street where a station opened in 1907. Plans for a light railway from the asbestos works at the bottom of Park Lane, alongside the canal and then beside the branch line which ran on an embankment, were put forward by Bell's Asbestos and Portland Cement in 1922, but met with opposition from Sir Francis Newdigate and never came to fruition.

The branch line ran through the grounds of Harefield Place. The mansion, having been sold in 1877 by Charles Newdigate-Newdegate to Henry Richard Cox, the banker who lived at Hillingdon House, was conveyed to the Cavendish Land Company in 1918 and sold on to George Rose the following year. He agreed with the GWGC Railway Company in 1928 to develop his land as a residential suburb if a new station were opened to serve it, guaranteeing a revenue of £1250 per year for five years. Harefield Halt, with a goods siding alongside, was opened on 24 September 1928 west of Harvil

176. Signboards advertising houses in Highfield Drive, to be built by W.S. Try, in 1938. The low stone wall surrounds the Gospel Oak, which marks the meeting point of Harefield and Hillingdon parishes.

177. The garden of Longwood, Harefield Place, in 1946.

Road. It was renamed South Harefield Halt in 1929. 25 trains stopped daily and 17 on Sundays. The suburb, however, only partially materialised, presumably because of financial difficulties. The shopping centres planned near the Halt and at New Years Green and Moorhall were not even started and the only residential building was fairly close to the mansion, along The Drive and in Highfield Drive. The railway company closed the station in 1931.

The Middlesex County Council, already concerned at the erosion of the county's last green spaces, bought 114 acres from George Rose the same year and leased them to Uxbridge Urban District Council in 1939 for use as a golf course – the farm where Richard Richardson the Quaker had once lived became the club house. A new club house was built subsequently, but some of the farm buildings still stand, though much altered. In 1938 the area become part of the Green Belt. The mansion was bought by the MCC in 1934 to become first a Convalescent Home for Women and Children, then in 1948, Uxbridge Convalescent Hospital and Uxbridge Country Hospital in 1951. After standing empty and in a shocking state for ten years after the closure of the hospital in 1969, it was bought by Estates and General Investments Ltd. Following careful restoration and conversion (including the addition of a horseshoe shaped building) it became the headquarters of the EBIC Division of the Dun and Bradstreet Corporation in 1985.

HAREFIELD: THE LAST VILLAGE IN MIDDLESEX

British United Asbestos Company began developing the 'Belfry Garden Village' in Belfry Avenue, just after the First World War, to provide accommodation for craftsmen among the workforce. Eight villas, all given aristocratic sounding names, were built in Belfry Avenue and some cottages by the chalk dell in Park Lane, but perhaps because of financial difficulties the 'village' plan was not fully realised. By 1923 the houses were being sold to the tenants and 9.6 acres went to the Uxbridge District Council.[2] Henry Clark, a carpenter purchased Ardrossan; Robert Collins, blacksmith, Silverlea; Sydney Pangbourne, plumber, Harewood; William Thrift, engine driver, Belmont and Henry Lintern, factory operator, West View.

Uxbridge Rural District Council and after 1929, the Urban District Council pursued a scattered housing policy in Harefield. More than 200 council houses were built between 1919-23; at Moorhall, on Mount Pleasant (the land taken from the Garden Village) down Park Lane and around the common. A further 273 went up between 1936-51; off Church Hill – St Mary's and St Anne's Roads; more at Mount Pleasant and around Northwood Road. Gilbert Road was built in the late 1950s. There was little private housing development near the village, because of the lack of commuter transport, but the coming of the M25 has made Harefield more desirable to home owners and much building activity has been started in the 1990s.

The village owes its retention of the old settlement pattern and nine working farms to the Middlesex County Council's Green Belt policy in the 1930s and the plea in Abercrombie's Greater London Plan (1944) to have the whole parish included in the Green Belt. The county council had already bought Langley, Knightscote and Bourne Farms from Mrs Tarleton's trustees, Park Lodge Farm from Sir Francis Newdigate-Newdegate and Whiteheath from the Stedall family in 1936. Highway and Dewes Farms also came into council possession. The Green Belt is under threat in 1995, with the Borough of Hillingdon attempting to deregulate part of the Breakspears estate near the stables with a view to converting them into cottages and probably building some extra houses nearby. Plans are also afoot to erect a new estate on the very site of Moorhall. There are grave doubts that the Unitary Development Plan will afford the protection originally intended to this last bastion of rural life.

178. *Council houses in Park Lane, Harefield.*

ICKENHAM – VILLAGE TO SUBURB

The 1382-acre Swakeleys estate was auctioned on Wednesday 5 July 1922, but it is not clear how much development was intended. Only five lots, mainly awkward pieces of fields which had been cut off by the railway line, were advertised as building land. The nine farms were mainly sold off in their entirety, some like Long Lane Farm being bought by Edward Dalton, the tenant and continued to be farmed. Not everything was sold. The mansion and 429-acre park was purchased in April 1923 by Mr Richard Cross of Little Manor Farm, Ruislip, farmer and Mr Frank Stedman of Guilford Street, London, Land Agent. They laid out new roads across the park, Warren Road, Swakeleys Drive (the old drive from Long Lane), Court Road, Milton Road, Ivy House Road, The Avenue (along the former drive from Back Lane) and Park Road (later Thornhill Road). The mansion and immediate parkland was sold to Mr Talbot and building plots were sold along the new roads and Swakeleys Road (the former Back Lane).

Stedman bought out Cross in 1924 and entered into a planning agreement with Uxbridge Urban District Council on 5 December 1924. Land along the River Pinn was to be conveyed to the Council five years after the date of the agreement, to be preserved as public open space. Only dwelling houses were to be built except for areas designated for shops at the bottom end of Swakeleys Road and on either side

of the proposed Western Avenue. The latter was part of Hercies Farm in Hillingdon. The average density of housing spread over the whole area was to be six to the acre and the area of each house was to be no more than one quarter of the total curtilage.

The West Middlesex Development Company entered into an agreement with Uxbridge Urban District Council in 1927, to develop the Ivy House Farm estate in accordance with the principles of a Town Planning Scheme then being prepared by the Council. Housing density was to be six to the acre along Swakeleys Road and twelve to the acre elsewhere. Hoylake Crescent, Wallesey Crescent, Bushey Road and Copthall Road East were laid out. The land along the Pinn was to be conveyed to the Council for public open space. The farm house and a particularly fine barn (listed), were demolished in 1964 at the same time as the old rectory – Alfred Pool had run a dairy herd and milk round from there.

Milton Farm and Church Farm continued as farms for some years, though with depleted amounts of land. By 1937 Ralph Potts Guy had acquired them and Tipper Farm and Ickenham Hall as well. The Milton Court Estate, advertised as Ickenham Garden City was begun in 1939. The farmhouse and a listed barn were demolished and a few houses erected, but most are post Second World War. Church Farm survived until 1946.

179. *The scene in Swakeleys Road in 1939, with Ivy House barn on the left and an advertisement for the Milton Court portion of Ralph Potts Guy's Ickenham Hall estate on the right.*

180. *'Ducky' Stent and his wife standing outside the White House in Glebe Avenue (then Marsh Lane) before 1922. Bythorne House now stands on the site.*

GREEN BELT

South of the railway line the lands of Manor Farm, the detached lands of Glebe Farm (owned by William Harries and not part of the Swakeleys estate) and Tipper Farm passed into the hands of Francis Jackson's development company. He was associated with George Ball who built the Manor Homes in Ruislip Manor. Plans were drawn up for a large housing estate replete with schools, cinema and shops. Sussex Road, Milverton Drive and Burnham Avenue were built or at least started before 1938, when the rest of the land except the site set aside for a school where Glebe Primary was built, became part of the Middlesex Green Belt. It remains so in the Borough of Hillingdon's Unitary Development Plan (draft 1993) except for the land bordering the Yeading Brook which is part of a 'green chain'. Francis Jackson's development company still own it. Houses were being built in Clovelly Close and Avenue by the Upjohn Construction Company in the 1950s, on the site of Glebe Farm.

WHITE HOUSE

A small holding in Glebe Avenue called the White House, occupied by Mrs Stent in 1922, was purchased by the Inwards family, who owned garages and Bythorne House now stands on the site.

LORDSHIP OF THE MANOR

Mr David Pool, tenant of Manor Farm before 1922, bought it and continued to live there. He paid £25 to Mr Stedman in 1927 for the lordship of the manor of Ickenham and after his death in 1956 his executors vested the lordship, which included rights over the green and marsh, in the borough of Uxbridge.

4MU WEST RUISLIP AND RAF RECORDS

Number 4 Maintenance Unit was opened near West Ruislip Station in 1917 on fields that were only a mile or so from Northolt Aerodrome. Mr Saich of Home Farm was contracted to provide horses and carts during the construction. The ground straddled the boundary between Ruislip and Ickenham and included Fairlight House, erected by Ernest A. Sims of Ickenham in 1914. The house still stands with Mr Sims' initials and the date on a plaque, and now houses the Commander of US Naval Activities, United Kingdom. Barracks, married quarters and RAF Records lay on the north side of the railway line and the maintenance sheds on the south. The sheds, being meant as temporary buildings, were only one brick thick with reinforcing columns, but were not pulled down as planned because of the Abyssinian crisis in the 1930s. Damaged propellers, ancillary engines and radar equipment were all repaired there during

181. Swakeleys Road was made into a dual-carriageway in 1936/7. The elms opposite Ivy House Farm, by the entrance to The Avenue were sacrificed.

182. The house built by Ernest Sims in 1914. Now called Fairlight House, it is the home of the US Naval Commander.

the Second World War. Trucks from the American 3rd Air Force European Forces Base at South Ruislip (opened Easter 1949) were also maintained there.

In 1975 the United States Navy leased the depot from the RAF and maintains services for US personnel within the base. There is a chapel, a child care centre and school, sports and fitness facilities, family housing units and a Medical and Dental Centre on Blenheim Crescent. The Baseball Diamond on the corner of Austins Lane and High Road is most obvious to passers by.

The oddly named Brackenbury Village (two miles from Brackenbury and not even remotely resembling a village) was built on part of the site in the 1980s.

HOME FARM AND THE VILLAGE CENTRE
Home Farm with its fine timber-framed house, stabling and dairy-shop alongside and barn in the field behind, spread an atmosphere of rural calm over Ickenham village centre until 1993. It was possible to walk down Austins Lane, stop by a gate and look back and see only the barn, field, farmhouse and the top of St Giles's steeple, with no signs of modern buildings and traffic lying so close. The field is now covered with large and attractive warden-controlled units called Church Place, a revival of the original name of Home Farm. The barn has been restored, but the rural aspect has gone for ever.

IMPORTANCE OF THE GREEN BELT
Both Harefield and Ickenham owe much of their charm to the fields, woods and open spaces that surround them and set them apart from the general run of suburbia. Even small, detached, and at present, derelict parts of the Green Belt, should be retained, for such areas can be revived. Once built upon, they are usually lost forever.

183. Ickenham pond being cleaned out in the 1930s.

Notes

The Two Parishes

1 Cotton, Mills and Clegg, *Archaeology in West Middlesex*, Hillingdon Borough Libraries (1986).
2 GLRO Acc 1085 EM9.
3 Worcester RO 009:1 BA 2636/148.
4 GLRO Acc 312/25 and Acc 312/16.

The Manors of Ickenham

1 Manorial background: *VCH Middlesex* Vol 4, pp 100-109.
2 *TLAMAS* 42 1991 pp 101-13 Patricia A. Clarke 'Ickenham Manor Farm'.
3 Information on the Shorediches comes mainly from GLRO Acc 425 1/1-7 and GLRO Acc 762 1-54.
4 GLRO MDR 1818 8 373.
5 Manorial information: *VCH Middlesex* Vol 4, pp 100-109.
6 Swakeleys Monograph, *Survey of London* (1933), Appendix A.
7 *Ibid*, Appendix C.
8 GLRO Acc 85 623.
9 GLRO Acc 1085 M 50.

The Manors of Harefield

1 C.A. Dowling, *The Lady Jane Dormer, Duchess de Feria 1538-1615*, Campion Books (1970).
2 Information re Lady Alice's family tree from Elona Cuthbertson *Gregory King's Harefield*, Hillingdon Borough Libraries (1992).
3 *Harefield History Society Newsletter* No 21: Elona Cuthbertson 'Lady Derby at home in Harefield 1634-5'.
4 GLRO Acc 1085 EM9.
5 GLRO MDR 1813 6 610.
6 Warwick RO CR 136 C2060.
7 GLRO Acc 1085 EF16
8 GLRO Acc 1085 EM1

St Giles's, Ickenham

1 PRO Prob 11 64.
2 Worcester RO 009:1 BA 2636/148.
3 GLRO Acc 85 347.

St Mary's, Harefield

1 *VCH Middlesex* Vol 3 pp 237-58.

2 Information on John Pritchett and his family from Elona Cuthbertson *Gregory King's Harefield*, Hillingdon Borough Libraries (1992).
3 *Ibid*.
4 GLRO Acc 1085 M74b.

Breakspears

1 *VCH Middlesex* Vol 3 p245.
2 PRO Cal SP dom 1603-10 151.
3 Documents penes Civic Centre, Uxbridge.

Harefield Park

1 GLRO MDR 1752 3 600.
2 PRO 272 Tray 42.
3 GLRO 1908 30 415.
4 Mary P. Shepherd *The Heart of Harefield*, Quiller Press (1990).

Lesser Estates

1 GLRO Acc 1085 M60
2 Elona Cuthbertson *Gregory King's Harefield*, Hillingdon Borough Libraries (1992).
3 Dorothy Winton in *Here and There in Harefield*, Harefield Extra-Mural Local History Class 1989.
4 Elona Cuthbertson *Gregory King's Harefield*, Hillingdon Borough Libraries (1992).
5 Much of the following information is taken from L.D. Jarvis & K. Meekcoms *The Story of Harefield House* (1982).
6 PRO Prob 11 948.
7 GLRO Acc 398 18.

Caring for the Poor

1 Elona Cuthbertson *Gregory King's Harefield*, Hillingdon Borough Libraries (1992).
2 *Ibid*.
3 H.S. Cochran ed. *Harefield Assessments*.
4 'The history of Harefield Workhouse' written by Dorothy Winton in *Harefield History Society Newsletters* Nos 18 and 19.
5 Harefield Almshouses: Charity Commissioners' Reports and Elona Cuthbertson *Gregory King's Harefield*

   Gell Almshouses: Morris W. Hughes *The Story of Ickenham*, Hillingdon Borough Libraries (1983).

Farming the Land

1 GLRO OBSR 227.
2 Geoffrey Tyack *Life and Work in a Middlesex Village*, Hillingdon Borough Libraries (1984).

Earning a Living

1 GLRO Acc 1085 M54.
2 GLRO MDR 1772 7 416.
3 PRO RAIL 830 38.
4 John Hassell *Tour of the Grand Junction Canal* (1819).
5 Harefield Local History Group *Harefield at that time of day* (1978).
6 GLRO MDR 1909 24 847.
7 GLRO MDR 1935 43 259.
8 GLRO MDR 1936 9 380.
9 GLRO MDR 1936 9 625.
10 GLRO MDR 1 603.
11 Harefield Rubber Co Ltd *The Harefield Story* (1970).
12 GLRO MDR 1909 27 516.
13 GLRO Acc 398 18.
14 Harefield Local History Group *Harefield at that time of day* (1978).

Chapels and Churches

1 Elona Cuthbertson *Gregory King's Harefield*, Hillingdon Borough Libraries (1992).
2 *VCH Middlesex* Vol 3 p256.

3 Uxbridge Library. Newspaper interview with James Milton, one of the trustees in 1927.
4 L.D. Jarvis *Free Church History of Uxbridge* (1953).
5 Morris W. Hughes *The Story of Ickenham* (1983).
6 GLRO Acc 762 34a and b
7 Information from Revd L. Keane.

Village Schools

1 *VCH Middlesex* Vol 3 p257.
2 *Ibid.*
3 Harefield Local History Group *Harefield at that time of day* (1978).
4 *VCH Middlesex* Vol 4 p108.
5 Grace Winch in *Ruislip, Northwood & Eastcote Local History Society Journal* (1984).
6 Morris W. Hughes *The Story of Ickenham*.

Village Life

1 Harefield Local History Group *Harefield at that time of day* (1978).
2 *Magnet* newspaper 27 July 1840.

The Changing Scene

1 Michael Dent in *Harefield History Newsletter* No. 21.
2 GLRO MDR 1923 7 210.

GLRO: *Greater London Record Office*; MDR: *Middlesex Deeds Registry*; PRO: *Public Record Office*; TLAMAS: *Transactions of the London and Middlesex Archaeological Society*; VCH: *Victoria County History*

The Illustrations

Illustrations have been reproduced with the kind permission of the following:

Aerofilms Ltd *84, 129*
Rev. D. Connor: *62*
Venetia Dalton: *38, 95, 120*
Hillingdon Heritage Services: *8, 16, 26, 27, 39, 41, 42, 44, 46, 49, 50, 51, 54, 55, 59, 68, 75, 80, 84, 85, 87, 93, 99, 100, 101, 102, 103, 104, 105, 118, 121, 124, 125, 129, 133, 135, 138, 142, 146, 154, 155, 157, 158, 168, 172, 173, 174, 176, 178, 179, 181*
L. Keane: *145*
The Linnean Society of London: *67*
National Monuments Record: *139*
Reg Neil, Harefield photographic historian: *12, 13, 35, 58, 60, 61, 63, 64, 66, 69, 72, 74, 81, 82, 83, 86, 89, 97, 98, 112, 116, 119, 123, 126, 127, 130, 131, 132, 134, 136, 137, 140, 147, 148, 149, 150, 151, 159, 161, 162, 164, 165, 170*
Peter Reed: *108*
R. Saich: *1, 28, 94, 153, 167, 169, 180, 183*
Karen Spink: *113*
United Reform Church, Ickenham: *141, 143, 144*
Grace Winch: *24*

The maps used in illustrations 2, 6, 11, 15 and 109 were drawn by the late D.F.A. Kiddle, and 111 by J. McBean.
All other illustrations were supplied by the author.